TEACHER'S PET PUBLICATIONS

PUZZLE PACK
for
The Contender
based on the book by
Robert Lipsyte

Written by
William T. Collins

© 2005 Teacher's Pet Publications
All Rights Reserved

The materials in this packet are copyrighted
by Teacher's Pet Publications, Inc.

These pages may be duplicated by the purchaser
for use in the purchaser's own classroom.

Copying any of these materials and distributing them
for any other purpose is a violation of the copyright laws.

© 2005 Teacher's Pet Publications, Inc.
www.tpet.com

INTRODUCTION
If you already own the LitPlan for this title, this Puzzle Pack will refresh your Unit Resource Materials and Vocabulary Resource Materials sections plus give you additional materials you can substitute into the tests. If you do not already have a complete LitPlan, these pages will give you some supplemental materials to use with your own plan. There are two main groups of materials: one set for unit words (such as characters' names, symbols, places, etc.) and one set for vocabulary words associated with the book.

WORD LIST
There is a word list for both the unit words and the vocabulary words. These lists show you which words are being used in the materials and the clues or definitions being used for those words. You may want to give students a word list with clues/definitions to help them, or you may want students to only have a word list (without clues/definitions) if you want them to work a little harder. Both are available for duplication. The word lists can also be your "calling key" for the bingo games.

FILL IN THE BLANK AND MATCHING
There are 4 each of the fill in the blank and matching worksheets for both the unit and vocabulary words. These pages can be used either as extra worksheets for students or as objective parts of a unit test. They can be done individually if students need extra help or as a whole class activity to review the material covered.

MAGIC SQUARES
The magic squares not only reinforce the material covered but also work on reasoning and math skills. Many teachers have told us that their students really enjoy doing these!

WORD SEARCH PUZZLES
The word search words go in all directions, as indicated on your answer keys. Two of the word search puzzles have the clues listed rather than the words. This makes the puzzle a little more difficult, but it reinforces the material better. Two word search puzzles have words only for students who find the clue puzzles too difficult.

CROSSWORD PUZZLES
Both unit and vocabulary word sections have 4 crossword puzzles.

BINGO CARDS
There are 32 individual bingo cards for the unit words and 32 individual bingo cards for the vocabulary words. You can use your word list as a "call list," calling the words at random and marking them off of your list as you go, or you could use the flash cards by cutting them apart and drawing the words at random from a hat (or box or whatever). To make a better review, you might ask for the definition and spelling of each word as you call it out–or you could call out the definitions and have students tell you the words they need to look for on the puzzle.

JUGGLE LETTERS
The vocabulary juggle letter game is intended to help students learn the spellings of the words. One sheet has the definitions listed on it as an extra help for students who need it or to reinforce the definitions if you choose to do so.

FLASH CARDS
We've included a set of vocabulary flash cards you can duplicate, cut, and fold for your students. Some teachers make a few sets for general use by the class; others make a set for each student. Some teachers duplicate them for each student and have the students cut & fold their own. You can cut out just the words and put them in a hat, have each student pick out one word and write the definition and a sentence for that word. Students then swap words and papers, with the next student adding a sentence of his own under the last one. You can have students swap as many times as you like. Each time the student will read the sentences written prior to his own and then add a sentence. You can cut out the words and definitions separately and play "I Have; Who Has?" Each student in the room draws a word and definition. The first student says, "I have (the name of the word). Who has the definition?" The student with the definition reads it then says, "I have (the name of the vocabulary word she has). Who has the definition?" The round continues until all words and definitions have been given.

Contender Word List

No.	Word	Clue/Definition
1.	ALARM	Alfred forgot to tell the gang about it
2.	ALFRED	The contender; he boxes and works
3.	BROOKS	Alfred's last name
4.	BUD	The 'cut man'; assistant manager
5.	CLIMBING	'It's the ____ that makes the man'
6.	CLUBHOUSE	Place where the gang meets
7.	CONTENDER	The ____
8.	DONATELLI	Boxing manager
9.	DOWN	'People will try to drag you ____'
10.	DRUGS	James was hooked on these
11.	EPSTEIN	Ex-fighter; Alfred's boss
12.	FEAR	'A man must have some ____'
13.	FRIENDS	Relationship between Alfred and James
14.	GRIFFIN	Alfred knocked him out in his 2nd fight
15.	GYM	Place to work out and practice boxing
16.	HENRY	Handicapped trainer and friend to Alfred
17.	HOLLIS	He, Major & Sonny beat up Alfred
18.	JAMES	Alfred's best friend
19.	JELLY	____ Belly; lacked self-discipline with food
20.	JOSE	Alfred knocked him down while sparring
21.	LIPSYTE	Author
22.	LYNN	Tried to recruit Alfred
23.	MADISON	____ Square Garden
24.	MAJOR	Bully; gang leader
25.	MIND	'You should have your own ____, do what you want'
26.	PARK	Place Alfred liked to run
27.	PEARL	Alfred's aunt
28.	PROMISED	'Nothing's ____ you, nothing's ever ____ you'
29.	SICK	How Alfred felt after his 2nd fight
30.	SOMEBODY	'Everybody is ____'
31.	SPOON	Ex-fighter; teacher
32.	STORE	Epstein's establishment
33.	TIMES	'____ are really changing'
34.	TRAINING	Practicing
35.	WALL	Alfred told his aunt a dog knocked him off a stone ____
36.	WILSON	He says to look for opportunities for the future

Contender Fill In The Blanks 1

_____
_____
_____
_____
_____
_____
_____
_____
_____
_____
_____
_____
_____
_____
_____
_____
_____
_____
_____
_____

1. The contender; he boxes and works
2. Practicing
3. Place Alfred liked to run
4. Ex-fighter; teacher
5. Alfred told his aunt a dog knocked him off a stone ____
6. He says to look for opportunities for the future
7. ____Belly; lacked self-discipline with food
8. 'A man must have some____'
9. Alfred's aunt
10. Handicapped trainer and friend to Alfred
11. Alfred knocked him down while sparring
12. Relationship between Alfred and James
13. How Alfred felt after his 2nd fight
14. 'It's the ____ that makes the man'
15. '____ are really changing'
16. ____ Square Garden
17. Alfred knocked him out in his 2nd fight
18. The____
19. Ex-fighter; Alfred's boss
20. He, Major & Sonny beat up Alfred

Contender Fill In The Blanks 1 Answer Key

ALFRED	1. The contender; he boxes and works
TRAINING	2. Practicing
PARK	3. Place Alfred liked to run
SPOON	4. Ex-fighter; teacher
WALL	5. Alfred told his aunt a dog knocked him off a stone ____
WILSON	6. He says to look for opportunities for the future
JELLY	7. ____Belly; lacked self-discipline with food
FEAR	8. 'A man must have some____'
PEARL	9. Alfred's aunt
HENRY	10. Handicapped trainer and friend to Alfred
JOSE	11. Alfred knocked him down while sparring
FRIENDS	12. Relationship between Alfred and James
SICK	13. How Alfred felt after his 2nd fight
CLIMBING	14. 'It's the ____ that makes the man'
TIMES	15. '____ are really changing'
MADISON	16. ____ Square Garden
GRIFFIN	17. Alfred knocked him out in his 2nd fight
CONTENDER	18. The____
EPSTEIN	19. Ex-fighter; Alfred's boss
HOLLIS	20. He, Major & Sonny beat up Alfred

Contender Fill In The Blanks 2

1. Alfred knocked him down while sparring
2. 'People will try to drag you____'
3. He, Major & Sonny beat up Alfred
4. The 'cut man'; assistant manager
5. 'You should have your own____, do what you want'
6. Epstein's establishment
7. Relationship between Alfred and James
8. ____ Square Garden
9. Tried to recruit Alfred
10. Ex-fighter; teacher
11. 'Everybody is ____'
12. Alfred knocked him out in his 2nd fight
13. 'A man must have some____'
14. Ex-fighter; Alfred's boss
15. James was hooked on these
16. Place to work out and practice boxing
17. The____
18. Alfred forgot to tell the gang about it
19. How Alfred felt after his 2nd fight
20. Alfred's aunt

Contender Fill In The Blanks 2 Answer Key

Answer	Clue
JOSE	1. Alfred knocked him down while sparring
DOWN	2. 'People will try to drag you____'
HOLLIS	3. He, Major & Sonny beat up Alfred
BUD	4. The 'cut man'; assistant manager
MIND	5. 'You should have your own____, do what you want'
STORE	6. Epstein's establishment
FRIENDS	7. Relationship between Alfred and James
MADISON	8. ____ Square Garden
LYNN	9. Tried to recruit Alfred
SPOON	10. Ex-fighter; teacher
SOMEBODY	11. 'Everybody is ____'
GRIFFIN	12. Alfred knocked him out in his 2nd fight
FEAR	13. 'A man must have some____'
EPSTEIN	14. Ex-fighter; Alfred's boss
DRUGS	15. James was hooked on these
GYM	16. Place to work out and practice boxing
CONTENDER	17. The____
ALARM	18. Alfred forgot to tell the gang about it
SICK	19. How Alfred felt after his 2nd fight
PEARL	20. Alfred's aunt

Contender Fill In The Blanks 3

_____ 1. Alfred's aunt

_____ 2. Ex-fighter; Alfred's boss

_____ 3. Relationship between Alfred and James

_____ 4. The____

_____ 5. Alfred forgot to tell the gang about it

_____ 6. Alfred knocked him out in his 2nd fight

_____ 7. '____ are really changing'

_____ 8. Handicapped trainer and friend to Alfred

_____ 9. Epstein's establishment

_____ 10. 'It's the ____ that makes the man'

_____ 11. 'A man must have some____'

_____ 12. James was hooked on these

_____ 13. Alfred told his aunt a dog knocked him off a stone ____

_____ 14. He says to look for opportunities for the future

_____ 15. The 'cut man'; assistant manager

_____ 16. Boxing manager

_____ 17. Alfred's last name

_____ 18. Ex-fighter; teacher

_____ 19. Place Alfred liked to run

_____ 20. 'Nothing's____you, nothing's ever ____ you'

Contender Fill In The Blanks 3 Answer Key

PEARL	1. Alfred's aunt
EPSTEIN	2. Ex-fighter; Alfred's boss
FRIENDS	3. Relationship between Alfred and James
CONTENDER	4. The ____
ALARM	5. Alfred forgot to tell the gang about it
GRIFFIN	6. Alfred knocked him out in his 2nd fight
TIMES	7. '____ are really changing'
HENRY	8. Handicapped trainer and friend to Alfred
STORE	9. Epstein's establishment
CLIMBING	10. 'It's the ____ that makes the man'
FEAR	11. 'A man must have some ____'
DRUGS	12. James was hooked on these
WALL	13. Alfred told his aunt a dog knocked him off a stone ____
WILSON	14. He says to look for opportunities for the future
BUD	15. The 'cut man'; assistant manager
DONATELLI	16. Boxing manager
BROOKS	17. Alfred's last name
SPOON	18. Ex-fighter; teacher
PARK	19. Place Alfred liked to run
PROMISED	20. 'Nothing's ____ you, nothing's ever ____ you'

Contender Fill In The Blanks 4

_____

_____

_____

_____

_____

_____

_____

_____

_____

_____

_____

_____

_____

_____

_____

_____

_____

_____

_____

_____

1. He says to look for opportunities for the future
2. James was hooked on these
3. Relationship between Alfred and James
4. How Alfred felt after his 2nd fight
5. Epstein's establishment
6. Place to work out and practice boxing
7. Place Alfred liked to run
8. 'A man must have some____'
9. The 'cut man'; assistant manager
10. Alfred's aunt
11. The____
12. 'You should have your own____, do what you want'
13. Alfred's best friend
14. Boxing manager
15. 'It's the ____ that makes the man'
16. Bully; gang leader
17. Alfred knocked him down while sparring
18. Ex-fighter; Alfred's boss
19. ____ Square Garden
20. Alfred's last name

Contender Fill In The Blanks 4 Answer Key

WILSON	1. He says to look for opportunities for the future
DRUGS	2. James was hooked on these
FRIENDS	3. Relationship between Alfred and James
SICK	4. How Alfred felt after his 2nd fight
STORE	5. Epstein's establishment
GYM	6. Place to work out and practice boxing
PARK	7. Place Alfred liked to run
FEAR	8. 'A man must have some____'
BUD	9. The 'cut man'; assistant manager
PEARL	10. Alfred's aunt
CONTENDER	11. The____
MIND	12. 'You should have your own____, do what you want'
JAMES	13. Alfred's best friend
DONATELLI	14. Boxing manager
CLIMBING	15. 'It's the ____ that makes the man'
MAJOR	16. Bully; gang leader
JOSE	17. Alfred knocked him down while sparring
EPSTEIN	18. Ex-fighter; Alfred's boss
MADISON	19. ____ Square Garden
BROOKS	20. Alfred's last name

Contender Matching 1

___ 1. SPOON   A. '____ are really changing'
___ 2. ALFRED   B. Practicing
___ 3. SICK   C. The contender; he boxes and works
___ 4. FEAR   D. James was hooked on these
___ 5. HENRY   E. 'You should have your own____, do what you want'
___ 6. CLIMBING   F. Alfred's aunt
___ 7. DRUGS   G. Tried to recruit Alfred
___ 8. GRIFFIN   H. He says to look for opportunities for the future
___ 9. TRAINING   I. Alfred knocked him out in his 2nd fight
___10. BROOKS   J. 'It's the ____ that makes the man'
___11. BUD   K. Place Alfred liked to run
___12. PARK   L. Handicapped trainer and friend to Alfred
___13. TIMES   M. Relationship between Alfred and James
___14. FRIENDS   N. How Alfred felt after his 2nd fight
___15. CONTENDER   O. The 'cut man'; assistant manager
___16. PEARL   P. Alfred told his aunt a dog knocked him off a stone ____
___17. DOWN   Q. Author
___18. JELLY   R. ____Belly; lacked self-discipline with food
___19. LYNN   S. Ex-fighter; Alfred's boss
___20. MIND   T. Ex-fighter; teacher
___21. WALL   U. 'A man must have some____'
___22. LIPSYTE   V. The____
___23. MADISON   W. ____ Square Garden
___24. WILSON   X. Alfred's last name
___25. EPSTEIN   Y. 'People will try to drag you____'

Contender Matching 1 Answer Key

T - 1. SPOON	A. '____ are really changing'
C - 2. ALFRED	B. Practicing
N - 3. SICK	C. The contender; he boxes and works
U - 4. FEAR	D. James was hooked on these
L - 5. HENRY	E. 'You should have your own____, do what you want'
J - 6. CLIMBING	F. Alfred's aunt
D - 7. DRUGS	G. Tried to recruit Alfred
I - 8. GRIFFIN	H. He says to look for opportunities for the future
B - 9. TRAINING	I. Alfred knocked him out in his 2nd fight
X - 10. BROOKS	J. 'It's the ____ that makes the man'
O - 11. BUD	K. Place Alfred liked to run
K - 12. PARK	L. Handicapped trainer and friend to Alfred
A - 13. TIMES	M. Relationship between Alfred and James
M - 14. FRIENDS	N. How Alfred felt after his 2nd fight
V - 15. CONTENDER	O. The 'cut man'; assistant manager
F - 16. PEARL	P. Alfred told his aunt a dog knocked him off a stone ____
Y - 17. DOWN	Q. Author
R - 18. JELLY	R. ____Belly; lacked self-discipline with food
G - 19. LYNN	S. Ex-fighter; Alfred's boss
E - 20. MIND	T. Ex-fighter; teacher
P - 21. WALL	U. 'A man must have some____'
Q - 22. LIPSYTE	V. The____
W - 23. MADISON	W. ____ Square Garden
H - 24. WILSON	X. Alfred's last name
S - 25. EPSTEIN	Y. 'People will try to drag you____'

Contender Matching 2

___ 1. GRIFFIN   A. Alfred told his aunt a dog knocked him off a stone ____
___ 2. BROOKS   B. Practicing
___ 3. TRAINING   C. Handicapped trainer and friend to Alfred
___ 4. DONATELLI   D. How Alfred felt after his 2nd fight
___ 5. MADISON   E. Epstein's establishment
___ 6. PROMISED   F. Alfred's best friend
___ 7. ALARM   G. Alfred's aunt
___ 8. ALFRED   H. 'Everybody is ____'
___ 9. BUD   I. 'Nothing's____you, nothing's ever ____ you'
___10. STORE   J. ____ Square Garden
___11. PEARL   K. Alfred forgot to tell the gang about it
___12. DOWN   L. Relationship between Alfred and James
___13. PARK   M. Place Alfred liked to run
___14. SPOON   N. Ex-fighter; teacher
___15. CLIMBING   O. Boxing manager
___16. SOMEBODY   P. Alfred knocked him down while sparring
___17. SICK   Q. Ex-fighter; Alfred's boss
___18. WALL   R. The contender; he boxes and works
___19. HOLLIS   S. Bully; gang leader
___20. EPSTEIN   T. 'People will try to drag you____'
___21. MAJOR   U. Alfred's last name
___22. JAMES   V. Alfred knocked him out in his 2nd fight
___23. JOSE   W. 'It's the ____ that makes the man'
___24. FRIENDS   X. The 'cut man'; assistant manager
___25. HENRY   Y. He, Major & Sonny beat up Alfred

Contender Matching 2 Answer Key

V - 1. GRIFFIN	A.	Alfred told his aunt a dog knocked him off a stone ____
U - 2. BROOKS	B.	Practicing
B - 3. TRAINING	C.	Handicapped trainer and friend to Alfred
O - 4. DONATELLI	D.	How Alfred felt after his 2nd fight
J - 5. MADISON	E.	Epstein's establishment
I - 6. PROMISED	F.	Alfred's best friend
K - 7. ALARM	G.	Alfred's aunt
R - 8. ALFRED	H.	'Everybody is ____'
X - 9. BUD	I.	'Nothing's ____ you, nothing's ever ____ you'
E -10. STORE	J.	____ Square Garden
G -11. PEARL	K.	Alfred forgot to tell the gang about it
T -12. DOWN	L.	Relationship between Alfred and James
M -13. PARK	M.	Place Alfred liked to run
N -14. SPOON	N.	Ex-fighter; teacher
W -15. CLIMBING	O.	Boxing manager
H -16. SOMEBODY	P.	Alfred knocked him down while sparring
D -17. SICK	Q.	Ex-fighter; Alfred's boss
A -18. WALL	R.	The contender; he boxes and works
Y -19. HOLLIS	S.	Bully; gang leader
Q -20. EPSTEIN	T.	'People will try to drag you ____'
S -21. MAJOR	U.	Alfred's last name
F -22. JAMES	V.	Alfred knocked him out in his 2nd fight
P -23. JOSE	W.	'It's the ____ that makes the man'
L -24. FRIENDS	X.	The 'cut man'; assistant manager
C -25. HENRY	Y.	He, Major & Sonny beat up Alfred

Contender Matching 3

___ 1. CONTENDER   A. How Alfred felt after his 2nd fight
___ 2. LIPSYTE   B. Alfred's aunt
___ 3. GRIFFIN   C. 'Nothing's____you, nothing's ever ____ you'
___ 4. SPOON   D. Handicapped trainer and friend to Alfred
___ 5. ALFRED   E. The____
___ 6. JAMES   F. Bully; gang leader
___ 7. DOWN   G. He says to look for opportunities for the future
___ 8. PROMISED   H. Place Alfred liked to run
___ 9. JOSE   I. The 'cut man'; assistant manager
___ 10. SOMEBODY   J. Ex-fighter; teacher
___ 11. SICK   K. Author
___ 12. PARK   L. Alfred's best friend
___ 13. PEARL   M. Tried to recruit Alfred
___ 14. BUD   N. Alfred knocked him out in his 2nd fight
___ 15. FRIENDS   O. 'Everybody is ____'
___ 16. LYNN   P. Alfred's last name
___ 17. BROOKS   Q. 'People will try to drag you____'
___ 18. MAJOR   R. 'You should have your own____, do what you want'
___ 19. DONATELLI   S. The contender; he boxes and works
___ 20. MIND   T. Place to work out and practice boxing
___ 21. MADISON   U. ____ Square Garden
___ 22. GYM   V. Relationship between Alfred and James
___ 23. WILSON   W. Boxing manager
___ 24. HENRY   X. 'It's the ____ that makes the man'
___ 25. CLIMBING   Y. Alfred knocked him down while sparring

Contender Matching 3 Answer Key

E - 1. CONTENDER	A.	How Alfred felt after his 2nd fight
K - 2. LIPSYTE	B.	Alfred's aunt
N - 3. GRIFFIN	C.	'Nothing's ____ you, nothing's ever ____ you'
J - 4. SPOON	D.	Handicapped trainer and friend to Alfred
S - 5. ALFRED	E.	The ____
L - 6. JAMES	F.	Bully; gang leader
Q - 7. DOWN	G.	He says to look for opportunities for the future
C - 8. PROMISED	H.	Place Alfred liked to run
Y - 9. JOSE	I.	The 'cut man'; assistant manager
O - 10. SOMEBODY	J.	Ex-fighter; teacher
A - 11. SICK	K.	Author
H - 12. PARK	L.	Alfred's best friend
B - 13. PEARL	M.	Tried to recruit Alfred
I - 14. BUD	N.	Alfred knocked him out in his 2nd fight
V - 15. FRIENDS	O.	'Everybody is ____'
M - 16. LYNN	P.	Alfred's last name
P - 17. BROOKS	Q.	'People will try to drag you ____'
F - 18. MAJOR	R.	'You should have your own ____, do what you want'
W - 19. DONATELLI	S.	The contender; he boxes and works
R - 20. MIND	T.	Place to work out and practice boxing
U - 21. MADISON	U.	____ Square Garden
T - 22. GYM	V.	Relationship between Alfred and James
G - 23. WILSON	W.	Boxing manager
D - 24. HENRY	X.	'It's the ____ that makes the man'
X - 25. CLIMBING	Y.	Alfred knocked him down while sparring

Contender Matching 4

___ 1. PEARL A. Place Alfred liked to run
___ 2. TRAINING B. Practicing
___ 3. HOLLIS C. Alfred knocked him down while sparring
___ 4. DOWN D. Alfred told his aunt a dog knocked him off a stone ____
___ 5. SICK E. Ex-fighter; teacher
___ 6. WALL F. Alfred's best friend
___ 7. JAMES G. Alfred's aunt
___ 8. LYNN H. How Alfred felt after his 2nd fight
___ 9. STORE I. Epstein's establishment
___ 10. CLIMBING J. Place to work out and practice boxing
___ 11. LIPSYTE K. 'You should have your own____, do what you want'
___ 12. FEAR L. 'People will try to drag you____'
___ 13. WILSON M. James was hooked on these
___ 14. CONTENDER N. He, Major & Sonny beat up Alfred
___ 15. JELLY O. Place where the gang meets
___ 16. GYM P. Author
___ 17. FRIENDS Q. He says to look for opportunities for the future
___ 18. MIND R. The____
___ 19. SPOON S. Boxing manager
___ 20. PARK T. 'A man must have some____'
___ 21. CLUBHOUSE U. Relationship between Alfred and James
___ 22. JOSE V. ____Belly; lacked self-discipline with food
___ 23. DRUGS W. Alfred forgot to tell the gang about it
___ 24. ALARM X. Tried to recruit Alfred
___ 25. DONATELLI Y. 'It's the ____ that makes the man'

Contender Matching 4 Answer Key

G - 1.	PEARL	A.	Place Alfred liked to run
B - 2.	TRAINING	B.	Practicing
N - 3.	HOLLIS	C.	Alfred knocked him down while sparring
L - 4.	DOWN	D.	Alfred told his aunt a dog knocked him off a stone ____
H - 5.	SICK	E.	Ex-fighter; teacher
D - 6.	WALL	F.	Alfred's best friend
F - 7.	JAMES	G.	Alfred's aunt
X - 8.	LYNN	H.	How Alfred felt after his 2nd fight
I - 9.	STORE	I.	Epstein's establishment
Y -10.	CLIMBING	J.	Place to work out and practice boxing
P -11.	LIPSYTE	K.	'You should have your own____, do what you want'
T -12.	FEAR	L.	'People will try to drag you____'
Q -13.	WILSON	M.	James was hooked on these
R -14.	CONTENDER	N.	He, Major & Sonny beat up Alfred
V -15.	JELLY	O.	Place where the gang meets
J -16.	GYM	P.	Author
U -17.	FRIENDS	Q.	He says to look for opportunities for the future
K -18.	MIND	R.	The____
E -19.	SPOON	S.	Boxing manager
A -20.	PARK	T.	'A man must have some____'
O -21.	CLUBHOUSE	U.	Relationship between Alfred and James
C -22.	JOSE	V.	____Belly; lacked self-discipline with food
M -23.	DRUGS	W.	Alfred forgot to tell the gang about it
W -24.	ALARM	X.	Tried to recruit Alfred
S -25.	DONATELLI	Y.	'It's the ____ that makes the man'

Contender Magic Squares 1

Match the definition with the vocabulary word. Put your answers in the magic squares below. When your answers are correct, all columns and rows will add to the same number.

A. STORE
B. SOMEBODY
C. FRIENDS
D. PROMISED
E. GYM
F. HOLLIS
G. TRAINING
H. CONTENDER
I. EPSTEIN
J. ALARM
K. DOWN
L. GRIFFIN
M. DRUGS
N. LYNN
O. MADISON
P. LIPSYTE

1. James was hooked on these
2. He, Major & Sonny beat up Alfred
3. The____
4. ____ Square Garden
5. Alfred knocked him out in his 2nd fight
6. Relationship between Alfred and James
7. Epstein's establishment
8. Alfred forgot to tell the gang about it
9. 'People will try to drag you____'
10. 'Nothing's____you, nothing's ever ____ you'
11. 'Everybody is ____'
12. Ex-fighter; Alfred's boss
13. Tried to recruit Alfred
14. Place to work out and practice boxing
15. Practicing
16. Author

A=	B=	C=	D=
E=	F=	G=	H=
I=	J=	K=	L=
M=	N=	O=	P=

Contender Magic Squares 1 Answer Key

Match the definition with the vocabulary word. Put your answers in the magic squares below. When your answers are correct, all columns and rows will add to the same number.

A. STORE
B. SOMEBODY
C. FRIENDS
D. PROMISED
E. GYM
F. HOLLIS
G. TRAINING
H. CONTENDER
I. EPSTEIN
J. ALARM
K. DOWN
L. GRIFFIN
M. DRUGS
N. LYNN
O. MADISON
P. LIPSYTE

1. James was hooked on these
2. He, Major & Sonny beat up Alfred
3. The____
4. ____ Square Garden
5. Alfred knocked him out in his 2nd fight
6. Relationship between Alfred and James
7. Epstein's establishment
8. Alfred forgot to tell the gang about it
9. 'People will try to drag you____'
10. 'Nothing's____you, nothing's ever ____ you'
11. 'Everybody is ____'
12. Ex-fighter; Alfred's boss
13. Tried to recruit Alfred
14. Place to work out and practice boxing
15. Practicing
16. Author

A=7	B=11	C=6	D=10
E=14	F=2	G=15	H=3
I=12	J=8	K=9	L=5
M=1	N=13	O=4	P=16

Contender Magic Squares 2

Match the definition with the vocabulary word. Put your answers in the magic squares below. When your answers are correct, all columns and rows will add to the same number.

A. SICK
B. TIMES
C. CONTENDER
D. HENRY
E. LYNN
F. TRAINING
G. MIND
H. BUD
I. PARK
J. MADISON
K. CLIMBING
L. ALFRED
M. FEAR
N. JAMES
O. EPSTEIN
P. LIPSYTE

1. The 'cut man'; assistant manager
2. How Alfred felt after his 2nd fight
3. '____ are really changing'
4. 'You should have your own____, do what you want'
5. ____ Square Garden
6. Ex-fighter; Alfred's boss
7. Author
8. Place Alfred liked to run
9. 'It's the ____ that makes the man'
10. Alfred's best friend
11. 'A man must have some____'
12. The contender; he boxes and works
13. Tried to recruit Alfred
14. Handicapped trainer and friend to Alfred
15. The____
16. Practicing

A=	B=	C=	D=
E=	F=	G=	H=
I=	J=	K=	L=
M=	N=	O=	P=

Contender Magic Squares 2 Answer Key

Match the definition with the vocabulary word. Put your answers in the magic squares below. When your answers are correct, all columns and rows will add to the same number.

A. SICK
B. TIMES
C. CONTENDER
D. HENRY
E. LYNN
F. TRAINING
G. MIND
H. BUD
I. PARK
J. MADISON
K. CLIMBING
L. ALFRED
M. FEAR
N. JAMES
O. EPSTEIN
P. LIPSYTE

1. The 'cut man'; assistant manager
2. How Alfred felt after his 2nd fight
3. '____ are really changing'
4. 'You should have your own____, do what you want'
5. ____ Square Garden
6. Ex-fighter; Alfred's boss
7. Author
8. Place Alfred liked to run
9. 'It's the ____ that makes the man'
10. Alfred's best friend
11. 'A man must have some____'
12. The contender; he boxes and works
13. Tried to recruit Alfred
14. Handicapped trainer and friend to Alfred
15. The____
16. Practicing

A=2	B=3	C=15	D=14
E=13	F=16	G=4	H=1
I=8	J=5	K=9	L=12
M=11	N=10	O=6	P=7

Contender Magic Squares 3

Match the definition with the vocabulary word. Put your answers in the magic squares below. When your answers are correct, all columns and rows will add to the same number.

A. GYM
B. FRIENDS
C. PEARL
D. MADISON
E. CONTENDER
F. STORE
G. LIPSYTE
H. JELLY
I. LYNN
J. ALFRED
K. JOSE
L. MAJOR
M. JAMES
N. WILSON
O. WALL
P. FEAR

1. He says to look for opportunities for the future
2. Author
3. Bully; gang leader
4. Place to work out and practice boxing
5. Alfred knocked him down while sparring
6. Relationship between Alfred and James
7. Alfred's best friend
8. ____Belly; lacked self-discipline with food
9. The____
10. 'A man must have some____'
11. Alfred's aunt
12. The contender; he boxes and works
13. ____ Square Garden
14. Tried to recruit Alfred
15. Epstein's establishment
16. Alfred told his aunt a dog knocked him off a stone ____

A=	B=	C=	D=
E=	F=	G=	H=
I=	J=	K=	L=
M=	N=	O=	P=

Contender Magic Squares 3 Answer Key

Match the definition with the vocabulary word. Put your answers in the magic squares below. When your answers are correct, all columns and rows will add to the same number.

A. GYM
B. FRIENDS
C. PEARL
D. MADISON
E. CONTENDER
F. STORE
G. LIPSYTE
H. JELLY
I. LYNN
J. ALFRED
K. JOSE
L. MAJOR
M. JAMES
N. WILSON
O. WALL
P. FEAR

1. He says to look for opportunities for the future
2. Author
3. Bully; gang leader
4. Place to work out and practice boxing
5. Alfred knocked him down while sparring
6. Relationship between Alfred and James
7. Alfred's best friend
8. ____Belly; lacked self-discipline with food
9. The____
10. 'A man must have some____'
11. Alfred's aunt
12. The contender; he boxes and works
13. ____ Square Garden
14. Tried to recruit Alfred
15. Epstein's establishment
16. Alfred told his aunt a dog knocked him off a stone ____

A=4	B=6	C=11	D=13
E=9	F=15	G=2	H=8
I=14	J=12	K=5	L=3
M=7	N=1	O=16	P=10

26
Copyrighted

Contender Magic Squares 4

Match the definition with the vocabulary word. Put your answers in the magic squares below. When your answers are correct, all columns and rows will add to the same number.

A. ALARM
B. HOLLIS
C. JELLY
D. LIPSYTE
E. JOSE
F. DRUGS
G. MIND
H. CLIMBING
I. CONTENDER
J. ALFRED
K. SICK
L. PEARL
M. SOMEBODY
N. EPSTEIN
O. BROOKS
P. PARK

1. James was hooked on these
2. The____
3. Alfred's last name
4. Author
5. 'Everybody is ____'
6. He, Major & Sonny beat up Alfred
7. 'It's the ____ that makes the man'
8. How Alfred felt after his 2nd fight
9. ____Belly; lacked self-discipline with food
10. Place Alfred liked to run
11. The contender; he boxes and works
12. Alfred knocked him down while sparring
13. Alfred's aunt
14. 'You should have your own____, do what you want'
15. Alfred forgot to tell the gang about it
16. Ex-fighter; Alfred's boss

A=	B=	C=	D=
E=	F=	G=	H=
I=	J=	K=	L=
M=	N=	O=	P=

Contender Magic Squares 4 Answer Key

Match the definition with the vocabulary word. Put your answers in the magic squares below. When your answers are correct, all columns and rows will add to the same number.

A. ALARM
B. HOLLIS
C. JELLY
D. LIPSYTE
E. JOSE
F. DRUGS
G. MIND
H. CLIMBING
I. CONTENDER
J. ALFRED
K. SICK
L. PEARL
M. SOMEBODY
N. EPSTEIN
O. BROOKS
P. PARK

1. James was hooked on these
2. The____
3. Alfred's last name
4. Author
5. 'Everybody is ____'
6. He, Major & Sonny beat up Alfred
7. 'It's the ____ that makes the man'
8. How Alfred felt after his 2nd fight
9. ____Belly; lacked self-discipline with food
10. Place Alfred liked to run
11. The contender; he boxes and works
12. Alfred knocked him down while sparring
13. Alfred's aunt
14. 'You should have your own____, do what you want'
15. Alfred forgot to tell the gang about it
16. Ex-fighter; Alfred's boss

A=15	B=6	C=9	D=4
E=12	F=1	G=14	H=7
I=2	J=11	K=8	L=13
M=5	N=16	O=3	P=10

Contender Word Search 1

Words are placed backwards, forward, diagonally, up and down. Clues listed below can help you find the words. Circle the hidden vocabulary words in the maze.

```
E S U O H B U L C L L N C W C W L Y W L
W F C R R M Y C Y O C K Z I Z J X G N M
B C B G N V W Y C C N C D L R V M W C Y
F F G J K S X B S H L T G S B S R H D J
R P J W C S F V O I N F E O D Q A P O J
P R O M I S E D M A J O R N W A L L N Z
B C J L S M B B E G S A E Y D Y A I A S
R K L A L Y I V B D E I S J N E E W T J
K O Q F M N H N O F R Z O N Y T R F E R
H P Y V G E G F D F N U J J S H J C L H
T A K B R Y S O Y Z B N G P F E P G L W
I R C H I M W R L C V G E S L N E J I M
M K D G F N F Z I G V Y D L B R A X P V
E Q D H F F F M P S Y M Y X R Y R N M S
S W Y W I R X H S X H K C C O G L A P Y
C M C Z N P Y G Y A N J R Y O N D O L Z
F V C L R R D N T P L R G K K I O Q W R
B U D J K R L J E F H F T G S N G Z Q C
R V L T V G L D R S H M R O W I H M K M
J L J B Z N B M O Y W H N E Y A C M R Y
K J S X F T V M T B S G N K D R V W Z Z
H L L M K D P P S C K W C H C T G Z D L
```

'A man must have some____' (4)
'Everybody is ____' (8)
'It's the ____ that makes the man' (8)
'Nothing's____you, nothing's ever ____ you' (8)
'People will try to drag you____' (4)
'You should have your own____, do what you want' (4)
'____ are really changing' (5)
Alfred forgot to tell the gang about it (5)
Alfred knocked him down while sparring (4)
Alfred knocked him out in his 2nd fight (7)
Alfred told his aunt a dog knocked him off a stone ____ (4)
Alfred's aunt (5)
Alfred's best friend (5)
Alfred's last name (6)
Author (7)
Boxing manager (9)
Bully; gang leader (5)
Epstein's establishment (5)

Ex-fighter; Alfred's boss (7)
Ex-fighter; teacher (5)
Handicapped trainer and friend to Alfred (5)
He says to look for opportunities for the future (6)
He, Major & Sonny beat up Alfred (6)
How Alfred felt after his 2nd fight (4)
James was hooked on these (5)
Place Alfred liked to run (4)
Place to work out and practice boxing (3)
Place where the gang meets (9)
Practicing (8)
Relationship between Alfred and James (7)
The 'cut man'; assistant manager (3)
The contender; he boxes and works (6)
The____ (9)
Tried to recruit Alfred (4)
____ Square Garden (7)
____Belly; lacked self-discipline with food (5)

Contender Word Search 1 Answer Key

Words are placed backwards, forward, diagonally, up and down. Clues listed below can help you find the words. Circle the hidden vocabulary words in the maze.

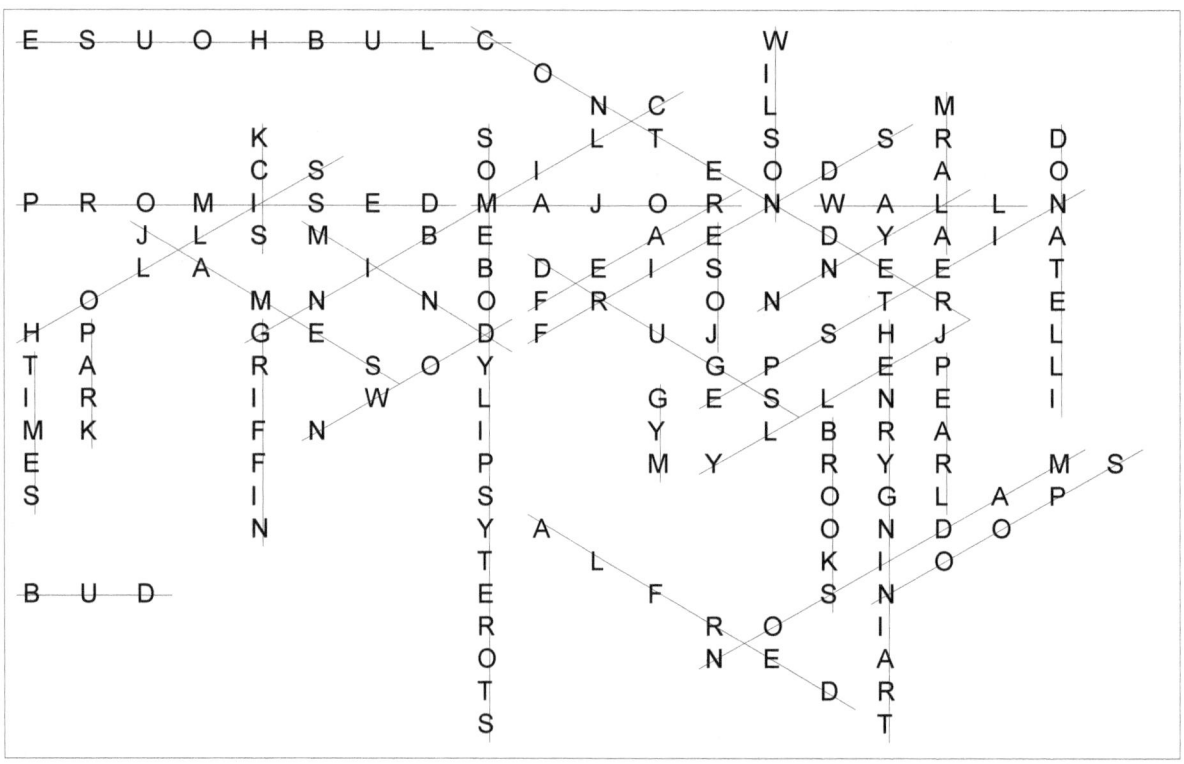

'A man must have some ____' (4)
'Everybody is ____' (8)
'It's the ____ that makes the man' (8)
'Nothing's ____ you, nothing's ever ____ you' (8)
'People will try to drag you ____' (4)
'You should have your own ____, do what you want' (4)
'____ are really changing' (5)
Alfred forgot to tell the gang about it (5)
Alfred knocked him down while sparring (4)
Alfred knocked him out in his 2nd fight (7)
Alfred told his aunt a dog knocked him off a stone ____ (4)
Alfred's aunt (5)
Alfred's best friend (5)
Alfred's last name (6)
Author (7)
Boxing manager (9)
Bully; gang leader (5)
Epstein's establishment (5)

Ex-fighter; Alfred's boss (7)
Ex-fighter; teacher (5)
Handicapped trainer and friend to Alfred (5)
He says to look for opportunities for the future (6)
He, Major & Sonny beat up Alfred (6)
How Alfred felt after his 2nd fight (4)
James was hooked on these (5)
Place Alfred liked to run (4)
Place to work out and practice boxing (3)
Place where the gang meets (9)
Practicing (8)
Relationship between Alfred and James (7)
The 'cut man'; assistant manager (3)
The contender; he boxes and works (6)
The ____ (9)
Tried to recruit Alfred (4)
____ Square Garden (7)
____ Belly; lacked self-discipline with food (5)

Contender Word Search 2

Words are placed backwards, forward, diagonally, up and down. Clues listed below can help you find the words. Circle the hidden vocabulary words in the maze.

```
A L F R E D D L Y P R S Z K D P X C Q F
Y P P Y Y Z B H M R R F G Y S S G M K T
D D H H J X B F P X L O D J P B Y B Z M
H Y C M F N L Z W R J X M W N M D V X B
V M J Y D S J Z S T F W V I H Z D S D Q
M L X D S J P C W Q Y N N H S N Y C B F
A J W X O S P H F Z S S D S C E H P R B
L X G Z T N G L J C P M X V S B D E O P
A M G B F N A H Y B O G J J I M M A O M
R Y A U K W N T P N O P F M C M V R K H
M I N D R U G S E Y N W O D K Y P L S Q
L C F Z I R C K Y L K B R N F M L D X H
Z C J G I S N T L L L N G W D A A G D Q
F M Q F J V O G S E M I T I W X Y J G W
J R F P O S Q N E J Y E P L V M K N O Y
X I I F S G L I M N G T L S W D I H D R
N D V E E C R B A Q B S H O Y N R O G Y
R F D R N A T M J P M P R N I T B L Z B
K W O C K D R I W A T E V A L E E L G G
T T C L S F S L W R R W R F M Y W I C R
S H E N R Y N C Y K P T R O Q W Z S C S
C O N T E N D E R B M E S U O H B U L C
```

'A man must have some____' (4)
'Everybody is ____' (8)
'It's the ____ that makes the man' (8)
'Nothing's____you, nothing's ever ____ you' (8)
'People will try to drag you____' (4)
'You should have your own____, do what you want' (4)
'____ are really changing' (5)
Alfred forgot to tell the gang about it (5)
Alfred knocked him down while sparring (4)
Alfred knocked him out in his 2nd fight (7)
Alfred told his aunt a dog knocked him off a stone ____ (4)
Alfred's aunt (5)
Alfred's best friend (5)
Alfred's last name (6)
Author (7)
Boxing manager (9)
Bully; gang leader (5)
Epstein's establishment (5)

Ex-fighter; Alfred's boss (7)
Ex-fighter; teacher (5)
Handicapped trainer and friend to Alfred (5)
He says to look for opportunities for the future (6)
He, Major & Sonny beat up Alfred (6)
How Alfred felt after his 2nd fight (4)
James was hooked on these (5)
Place Alfred liked to run (4)
Place to work out and practice boxing (3)
Place where the gang meets (9)
Practicing (8)
Relationship between Alfred and James (7)
The 'cut man'; assistant manager (3)
The contender; he boxes and works (6)
The____ (9)
Tried to recruit Alfred (4)
____ Square Garden (7)
____Belly; lacked self-discipline with food (5)

Contender Word Search 2 Answer Key

Words are placed backwards, forward, diagonally, up and down. Clues listed below can help you find the words. Circle the hidden vocabulary words in the maze.

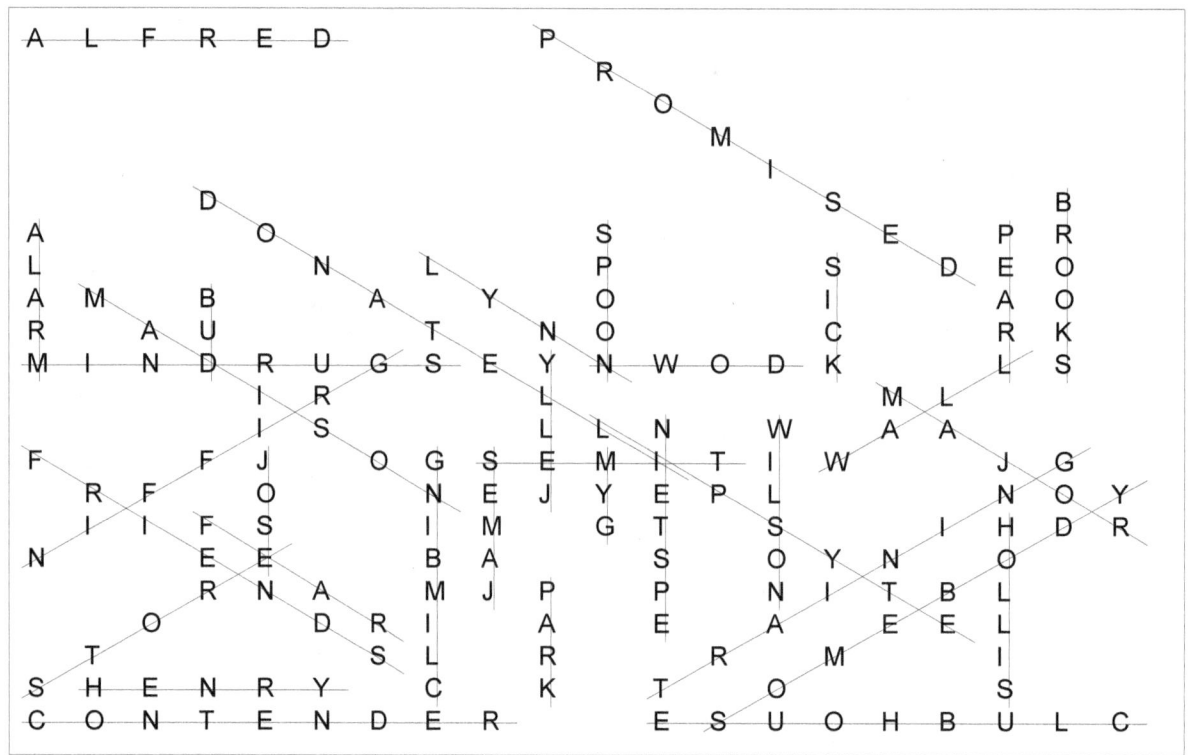

'A man must have some____' (4)
'Everybody is ____' (8)
'It's the ____ that makes the man' (8)
'Nothing's____you, nothing's ever ____ you' (8)
'People will try to drag you____' (4)
'You should have your own____, do what you want' (4)
'____ are really changing' (5)
Alfred forgot to tell the gang about it (5)
Alfred knocked him down while sparring (4)
Alfred knocked him out in his 2nd fight (7)
Alfred told his aunt a dog knocked him off a stone ____ (4)
Alfred's aunt (5)
Alfred's best friend (5)
Alfred's last name (6)
Author (7)
Boxing manager (9)
Bully; gang leader (5)
Epstein's establishment (5)

Ex-fighter; Alfred's boss (7)
Ex-fighter; teacher (5)
Handicapped trainer and friend to Alfred (5)
He says to look for opportunities for the future (6)
He, Major & Sonny beat up Alfred (6)
How Alfred felt after his 2nd fight (4)
James was hooked on these (5)
Place Alfred liked to run (4)
Place to work out and practice boxing (3)
Place where the gang meets (9)
Practicing (8)
Relationship between Alfred and James (7)
The 'cut man'; assistant manager (3)
The contender; he boxes and works (6)
The____ (9)
Tried to recruit Alfred (4)
____ Square Garden (7)
____Belly; lacked self-discipline with food (5)

Contender Word Search 3

Words are placed backwards, forward, diagonally, up and down. Words listed below are included in the maze. Circle the hidden vocabulary words in the maze.

```
C R F K D C H D P R O M I S E D P N H F
N C R T T F W K G C T H C L Y B G T F S
J A F P R S W H B L L Z F W G D R S G J
P B Z H H A C D K I W V A W K Z I J V C
V S G B X D I G H M X K L B C Y F M F P
Y Z N P Q W X N F B L R A Q X N F H J C
D F Z X P Z G H I I M L R V M Y I D O Y
O F S G M F R I E N D S M I N D N J S V
B K E H B M T S N G G A K J Q W H I E L
E Q K A F Y V Y G W D S W X E A L J P Z
M A J O R M L K E I T I M E S L K Q S L
O R R N W S V R S L C C J M O L L E T G
S W E B S L O O F S I K X H X Q M Y E G
T H D R H T N V X O R P D Z Z A F D I S
D X N O S D L B J N F F S R J V Z O N T
R W E O Z O C Q O B B S M Y U Q Z N R C
K F T K Y W G O M U N J P J T G P A R N
C W N S G N P M M D E R F L A E S T J P
C G O R S S Y H C Z X W B M A V J E Z D
H F C N L G V Y X Z M J R R P T J L X K
P L Q G H K P D W Y W N L K V Q P L G P
C L U B H O U S E T B P C F M L F I Y Z
```

ALARM	DRUGS	JELLY	PROMISED
ALFRED	EPSTEIN	JOSE	SICK
BROOKS	FEAR	LIPSYTE	SOMEBODY
BUD	FRIENDS	LYNN	SPOON
CLIMBING	GRIFFIN	MADISON	STORE
CLUBHOUSE	GYM	MAJOR	TIMES
CONTENDER	HENRY	MIND	TRAINING
DONATELLI	HOLLIS	PARK	WALL
DOWN	JAMES	PEARL	WILSON

Contender Word Search 3 Answer Key

Words are placed backwards, forward, diagonally, up and down. Words listed below are included in the maze. Circle the hidden vocabulary words in the maze.

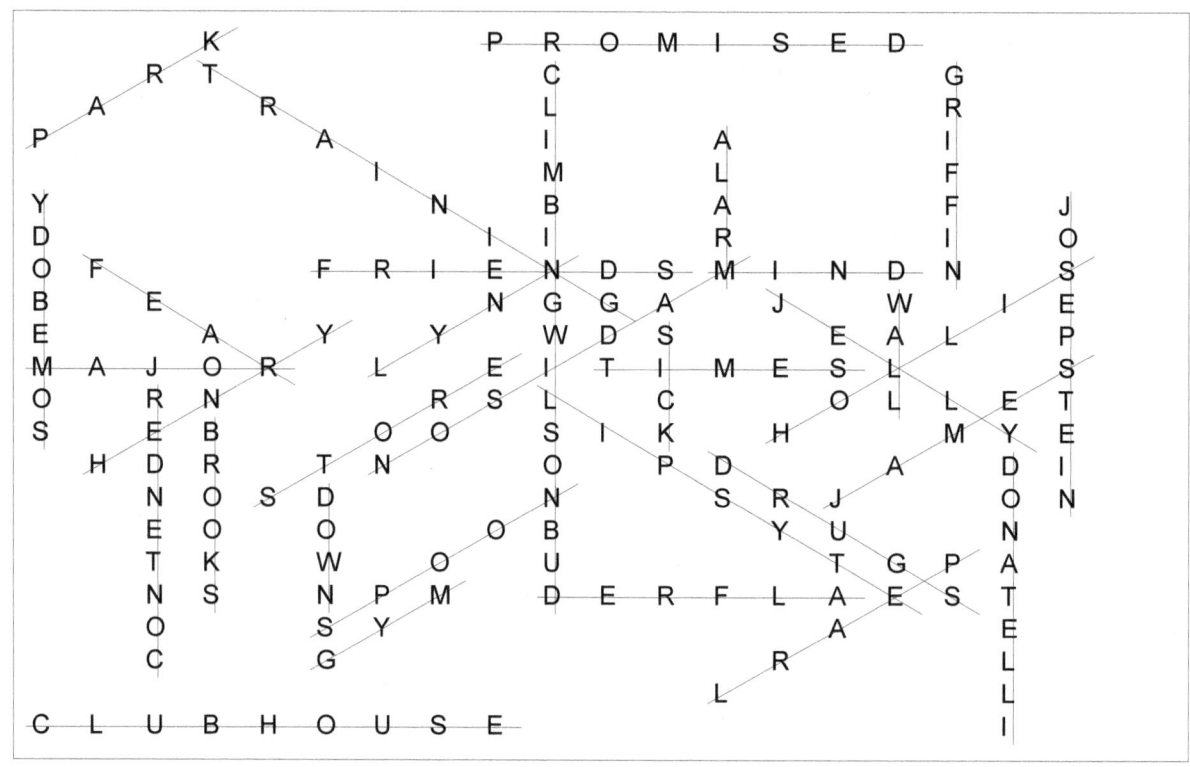

ALARM	DRUGS	JELLY	PROMISED
ALFRED	EPSTEIN	JOSE	SICK
BROOKS	FEAR	LIPSYTE	SOMEBODY
BUD	FRIENDS	LYNN	SPOON
CLIMBING	GRIFFIN	MADISON	STORE
CLUBHOUSE	GYM	MAJOR	TIMES
CONTENDER	HENRY	MIND	TRAINING
DONATELLI	HOLLIS	PARK	WALL
DOWN	JAMES	PEARL	WILSON

Contender Word Search 4

Words are placed backwards, forward, diagonally, up and down. Words listed below are included in the maze. Circle the hidden vocabulary words in the maze.

```
P L R Y H Z D S V E C A S V N V L A F G
F D E S I M O R P H O L L I S N L E N R
T N D R S B O S U O J C U F N A A R F R
D I N R N J T P K G O A V B R R W O D F
B M E L A E F H D L S N M M H E R T Z V
N N T M I H E N R Y I W S E B O D S Y R
D B N N D D Z R T L K D I W S Z U X S H
O B O Y T G G X L L N M M L N J Z S V H
W R C L H H Y E T E J N K S S Z K S E B
N L M B K S T M I J S O M E B O D Y P G
W P G R S A X R M L T S J G O X N L Y B
T T A K N R F D E K T I R R M H Y H T
G P D O Q J B Z S B Y D B T M I T N V P
T B D U B Q M K Z P L A B J Z R F N G Z
G R B Z B G C Y T R R M J X O G W F J G
M L A L Z I T L A C V P J W H S P W I P
T G H I S L Y E I M G L L N Q P E L F N
G X M P N D P C G M W N Y R J S S B B Q
K S Y S B I F V X N B J C K V K X L B L
H V F Y H C N X M K V I B K N S L X X X
D J R T V S V G K G M R N H K M H L P Z
J D Q E P G M S X T N N Z G M N F M M M
```

ALARM	DRUGS	JELLY	PROMISED
ALFRED	EPSTEIN	JOSE	SICK
BROOKS	FEAR	LIPSYTE	SOMEBODY
BUD	FRIENDS	LYNN	SPOON
CLIMBING	GRIFFIN	MADISON	STORE
CLUBHOUSE	GYM	MAJOR	TIMES
CONTENDER	HENRY	MIND	TRAINING
DONATELLI	HOLLIS	PARK	WALL
DOWN	JAMES	PEARL	WILSON

Contender Word Search 4 Answer Key

Words are placed backwards, forward, diagonally, up and down. Words listed below are included in the maze. Circle the hidden vocabulary words in the maze.

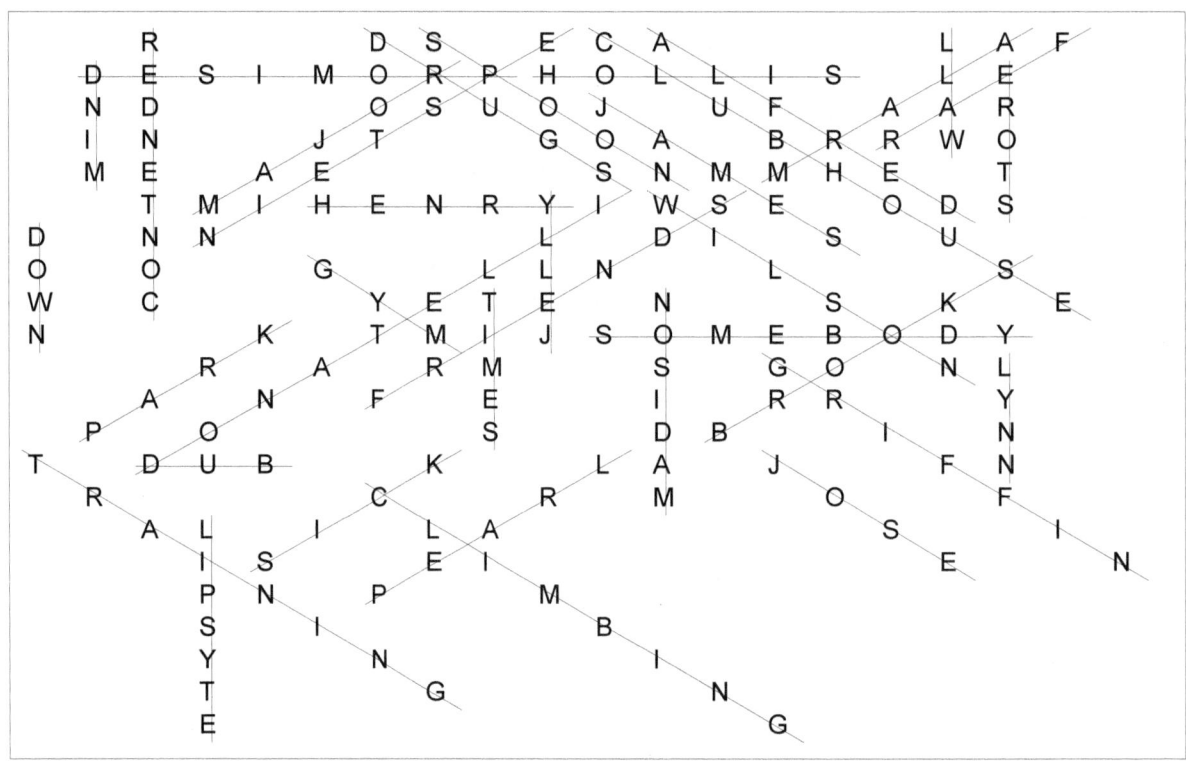

ALARM	DRUGS	JELLY	PROMISED
ALFRED	EPSTEIN	JOSE	SICK
BROOKS	FEAR	LIPSYTE	SOMEBODY
BUD	FRIENDS	LYNN	SPOON
CLIMBING	GRIFFIN	MADISON	STORE
CLUBHOUSE	GYM	MAJOR	TIMES
CONTENDER	HENRY	MIND	TRAINING
DONATELLI	HOLLIS	PARK	WALL
DOWN	JAMES	PEARL	WILSON

Contender Crossword 1

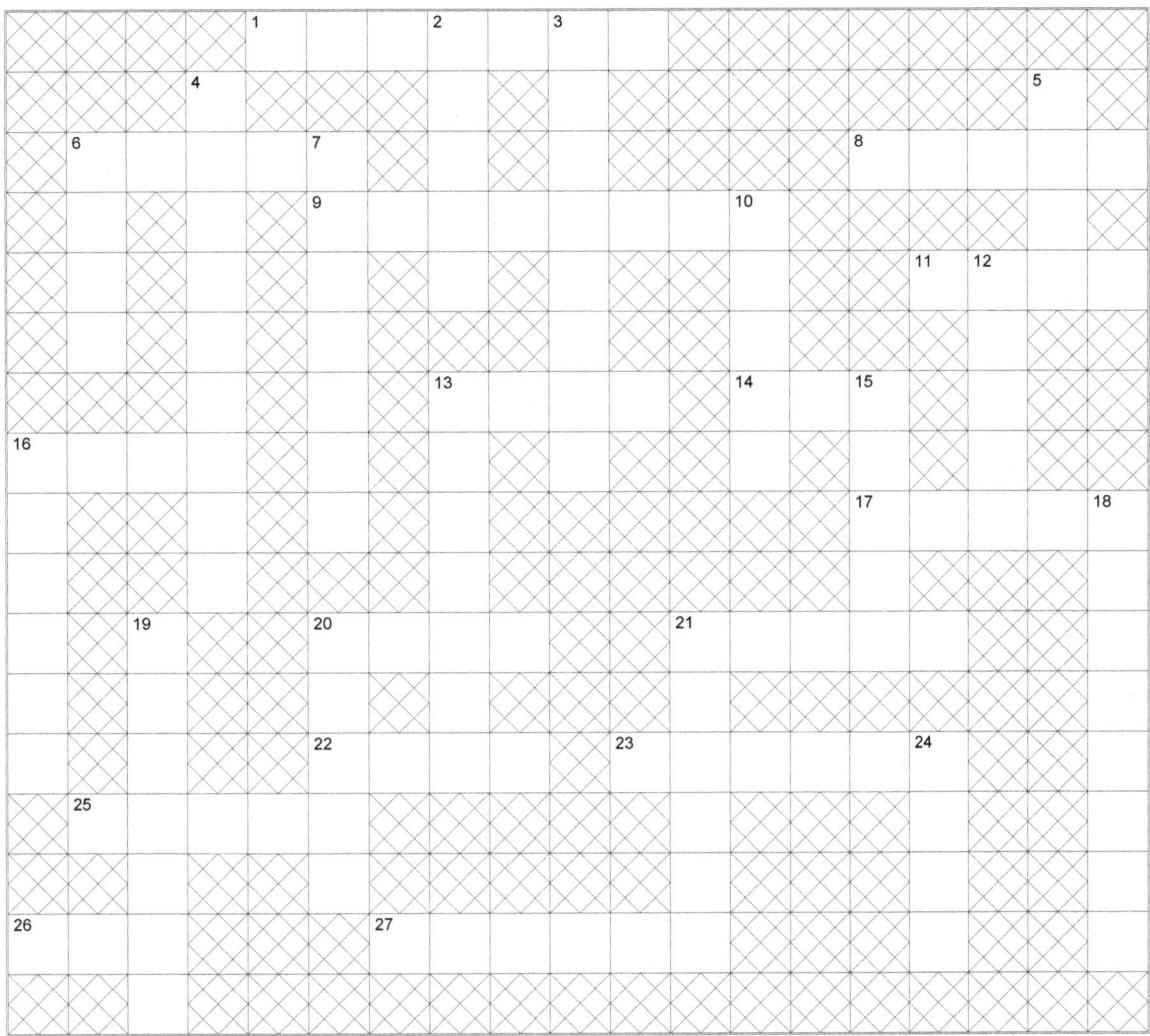

Across
1. Author
6. Epstein's establishment
8. '____ are really changing'
9. 'Nothing's____you, nothing's ever ____ you'
11. Place Alfred liked to run
13. 'You should have your own____, do what you want'
14. Place to work out and practice boxing
16. Alfred told his aunt a dog knocked him off a stone ____
17. Alfred's best friend
20. Alfred knocked him down while sparring
21. Handicapped trainer and friend to Alfred
22. Tried to recruit Alfred
23. The contender; he boxes and works
25. Alfred's aunt
26. The 'cut man'; assistant manager
27. Alfred's last name

Down
2. Ex-fighter; teacher
3. Practicing
4. Boxing manager
5. 'A man must have some____'
6. How Alfred felt after his 2nd fight
7. Ex-fighter; Alfred's boss
10. James was hooked on these
12. Alfred forgot to tell the gang about it
13. ____ Square Garden
15. Bully; gang leader
16. He says to look for opportunities for the future
18. 'Everybody is ____'
19. Relationship between Alfred and James
20. ____Belly; lacked self-discipline with food
21. He, Major & Sonny beat up Alfred
24. 'People will try to drag you____'

Contender Crossword 1 Answer Key

			1 L	I	2 P S	Y	3 T E						
		4 D			P		R					5 F	
6 S	7 T	O	R	E		O		A		8 T	I	M	E	S
	I	N		9 P	R	O	M	I	S	E	10 D		A	
	C	A		S		N		N			R	11 P	12 A	R	K
	K	T		T				I			U		L	
		E		E		13 M	I	N	D		14 G	15 Y M	A	
16 W	A	L	L		I	A		G			S	A	R	
I		L		N		D						17 J	A	M	E	18 S
L		I				I						O			O
S	19 F		20 J	O	S	E		21 H	E	N	R	Y			M
O	R		E			O		O						E
N	I		22 L	Y	N	N		23 A	L	F	24 R	E	D		B
	25 P	E	A	R	L			L			O		O
	N			Y				I			W		D
26 B	U	D		27 B	R	O	O	K	S		N		Y
	S												

Across
1. Author
6. Epstein's establishment
8. '____ are really changing'
9. 'Nothing's____you, nothing's ever ____ you'
11. Place Alfred liked to run
13. 'You should have your own____, do what you want'
14. Place to work out and practice boxing
16. Alfred told his aunt a dog knocked him off a stone ____
17. Alfred's best friend
20. Alfred knocked him down while sparring
21. Handicapped trainer and friend to Alfred
22. Tried to recruit Alfred
23. The contender; he boxes and works
25. Alfred's aunt
26. The 'cut man'; assistant manager
27. Alfred's last name

Down
2. Ex-fighter; teacher
3. Practicing
4. Boxing manager
5. 'A man must have some____'
6. How Alfred felt after his 2nd fight
7. Ex-fighter; Alfred's boss
10. James was hooked on these
12. Alfred forgot to tell the gang about it
13. ____ Square Garden
15. Bully; gang leader
16. He says to look for opportunities for the future
18. 'Everybody is ____'
19. Relationship between Alfred and James
20. ____Belly; lacked self-discipline with food
21. He, Major & Sonny beat up Alfred
24. 'People will try to drag you____'

Contender Crossword 2

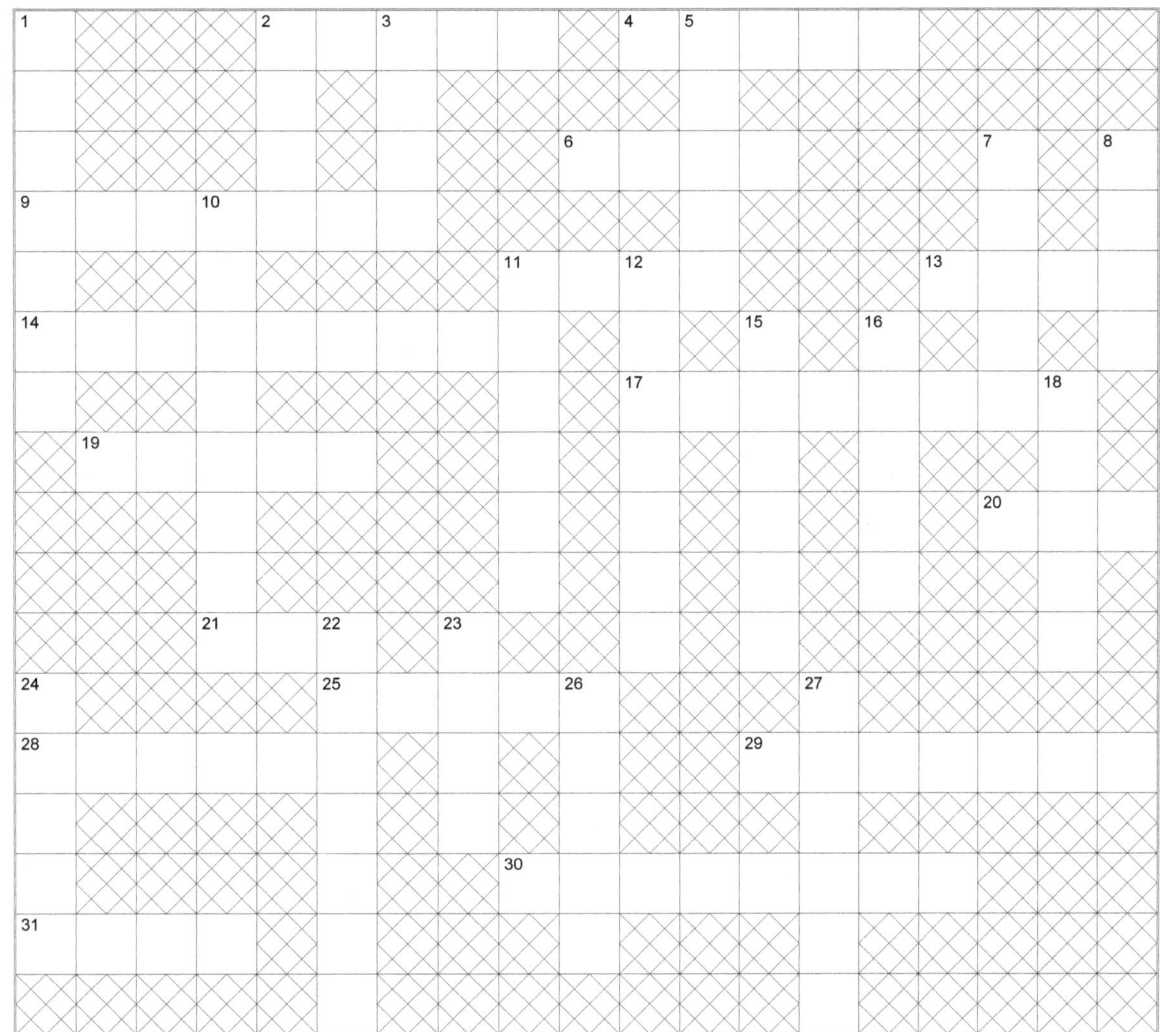

Across
2. ____Belly; lacked self-discipline with food
4. Ex-fighter; teacher
6. 'A man must have some____'
9. Ex-fighter; Alfred's boss
11. Alfred told his aunt a dog knocked him off a stone ____
13. 'People will try to drag you____'
14. Boxing manager
17. 'Nothing's____you, nothing's ever ____ you'
19. Handicapped trainer and friend to Alfred
20. The 'cut man'; assistant manager
21. Place to work out and practice boxing
25. Alfred forgot to tell the gang about it
28. The contender; he boxes and works
29. Alfred knocked him out in his 2nd fight
30. 'Everybody is ____'
31. How Alfred felt after his 2nd fight

Down
1. Relationship between Alfred and James
2. Alfred knocked him down while sparring
3. Tried to recruit Alfred
5. Alfred's aunt
7. Epstein's establishment
8. 'You should have your own____, do what you want'
10. Practicing
11. He says to look for opportunities for the future
12. Author
15. He, Major & Sonny beat up Alfred
16. '____ are really changing'
18. James was hooked on these
22. ____ Square Garden
23. Place Alfred liked to run
24. Alfred's best friend
26. Bully; gang leader
27. Alfred's last name

Contender Crossword 2 Answer Key

	1 F			2 J	3 E	L	L	Y		4 S	5 P	O	O	N		
	R			O		Y					E					
	I			S		N			6 F	E	A	R		7 S		8 M
9 E	P	S	10 T	E	I	N					R			T		I
	N		R				11 W	12 A	L	L			13 D	O	W	N
14 D	O	N	A	T	E	L	L	I		15 H	16 T		R		18 D
S		I					L	17 P	R	O	M	I	S	E	D
		19 H	E	N	R	Y		S	S	L	M		R	
		I					S	Y	L	E	20 B	U	D
		N					N	T	I	S		G	
			21 G	22 Y	M	23 P		E	S			S	
24 J			25 A	L	A	R	26 M		27 B			
28 A	L	F	R	E	D		R		A		29 G	R	I	F	F	I	N
M			I		K		J		O			
E			S		30 S	O	M	E	B	O	D	Y
31 S	I	C	K		O		R		K			
					N				S			

Across
2. ____Belly; lacked self-discipline with food
4. Ex-fighter; teacher
6. 'A man must have some____'
9. Ex-fighter; Alfred's boss
11. Alfred told his aunt a dog knocked him off a stone ____
13. 'People will try to drag you____'
14. Boxing manager
17. 'Nothing's____you, nothing's ever ____ you'
19. Handicapped trainer and friend to Alfred
20. The 'cut man'; assistant manager
21. Place to work out and practice boxing
25. Alfred forgot to tell the gang about it
28. The contender; he boxes and works
29. Alfred knocked him out in his 2nd fight
30. 'Everybody is ____'
31. How Alfred felt after his 2nd fight

Down
1. Relationship between Alfred and James
2. Alfred knocked him down while sparring
3. Tried to recruit Alfred
5. Alfred's aunt
7. Epstein's establishment
8. 'You should have your own____, do what you want'
10. Practicing
11. He says to look for opportunities for the future
12. Author
15. He, Major & Sonny beat up Alfred
16. '____ are really changing'
18. James was hooked on these
22. ____ Square Garden
23. Place Alfred liked to run
24. Alfred's best friend
26. Bully; gang leader
27. Alfred's last name

Contender Crossword 3

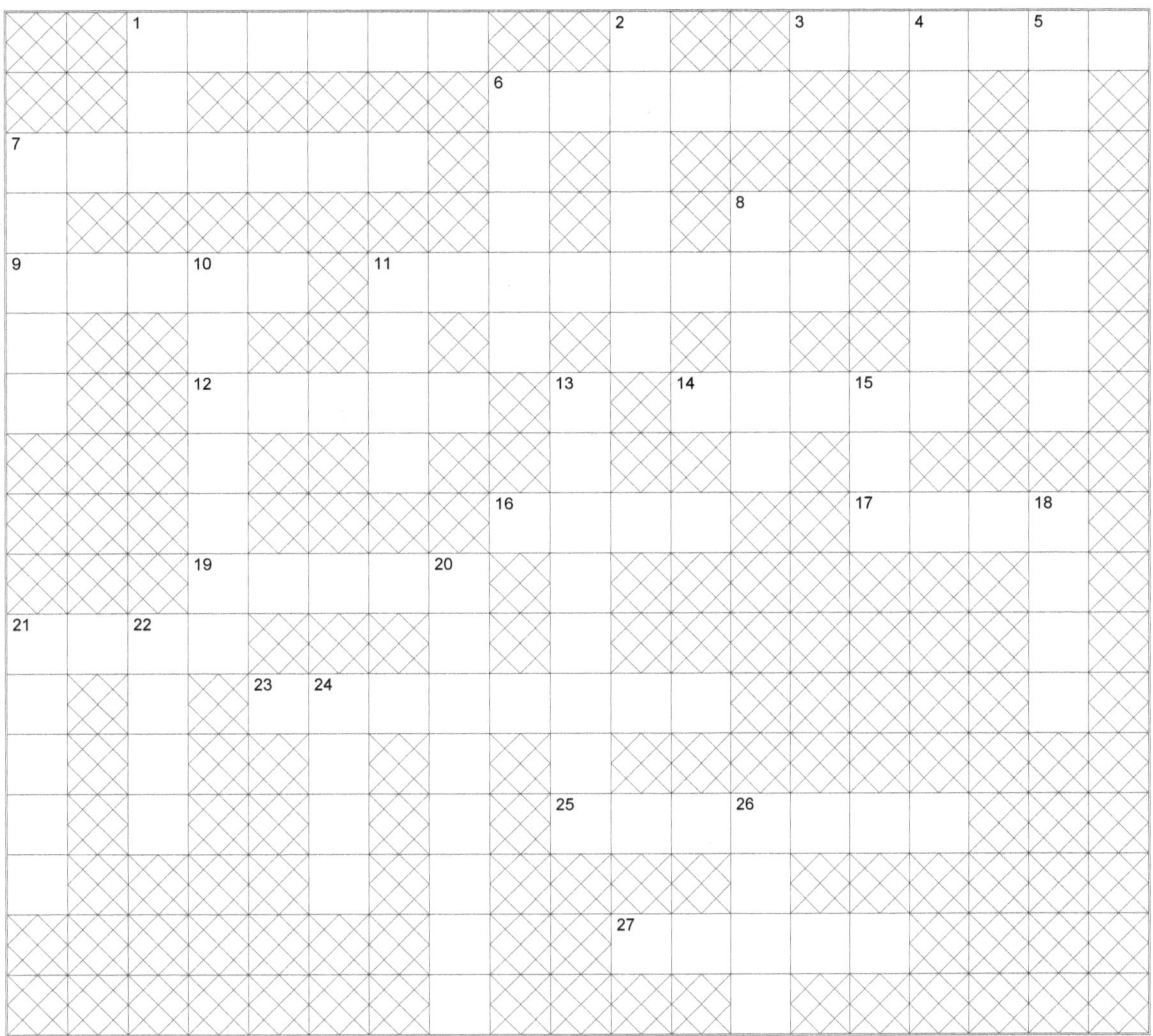

Across
1. Alfred's last name
3. The contender; he boxes and works
6. Epstein's establishment
7. ____ Square Garden
9. ____Belly; lacked self-discipline with food
11. 'Nothing's____you, nothing's ever ____ you'
12. Alfred's aunt
14. James was hooked on these
16. Alfred told his aunt a dog knocked him off a stone ____
17. 'You should have your own____, do what you want'
19. '____ are really changing'
21. Alfred knocked him down while sparring
23. 'It's the ____ that makes the man'
25. Alfred knocked him out in his 2nd fight
27. Alfred forgot to tell the gang about it

Down
1. The 'cut man'; assistant manager
2. He, Major & Sonny beat up Alfred
4. Relationship between Alfred and James
5. Ex-fighter; Alfred's boss
6. Ex-fighter; teacher
7. Bully; gang leader
8. Handicapped trainer and friend to Alfred
10. Author
11. Place Alfred liked to run
13. Practicing
15. Place to work out and practice boxing
18. 'People will try to drag you____'
20. 'Everybody is ____'
21. Alfred's best friend
22. How Alfred felt after his 2nd fight
24. Tried to recruit Alfred
26. 'A man must have some____'

Contender Crossword 3 Answer Key

		1 B	R	O	O	K	S			2 H			3 A	4 L	5 F	R	E	D
		U							6 S	T	O	R	E		R		P	
7 M	A	D	I	S	O	N		P		L					I		S	
A						O		L		H			8		E		T	
9 J	E	10 L	L	Y		11 P	R	O	M	I	S	E	D		N		E	
O		I				A		N		S		N			D		I	
R		12 P	E	A	R	L		13 T		14 D	R	U	15 G	S			N	
		S				K		R		Y			Y					
		Y						16 W	A	L	L		17 M	I	18 N	D		
				19 T	I	M	20 E	S		I					O			
21 J	22 O	S	E				O			N					W			
A		I		23 C	24 L	I	M	B	I	N	G				N			
M		C			Y		E											
E		K					B		25 G	R	I	26 F	F	I	N			
S							O					E						
							D		27 A	L	A	R	M					
							Y					R						

Across
1. Alfred's last name
3. The contender; he boxes and works
6. Epstein's establishment
7. ____ Square Garden
9. ____Belly; lacked self-discipline with food
11. 'Nothing's____ you, nothing's ever ____ you'
12. Alfred's aunt
14. James was hooked on these
16. Alfred told his aunt a dog knocked him off a stone ____
17. 'You should have your own____, do what you want'
19. '____ are really changing'
21. Alfred knocked him down while sparring
23. 'It's the ____ that makes the man'
25. Alfred knocked him out in his 2nd fight
27. Alfred forgot to tell the gang about it

Down
1. The 'cut man'; assistant manager
2. He, Major & Sonny beat up Alfred
4. Relationship between Alfred and James
5. Ex-fighter; Alfred's boss
6. Ex-fighter; teacher
7. Bully; gang leader
8. Handicapped trainer and friend to Alfred
10. Author
11. Place Alfred liked to run
13. Practicing
15. Place to work out and practice boxing
18. 'People will try to drag you____'
20. 'Everybody is ____'
21. Alfred's best friend
22. How Alfred felt after his 2nd fight
24. Tried to recruit Alfred
26. 'A man must have some____'

Contender Crossword 4

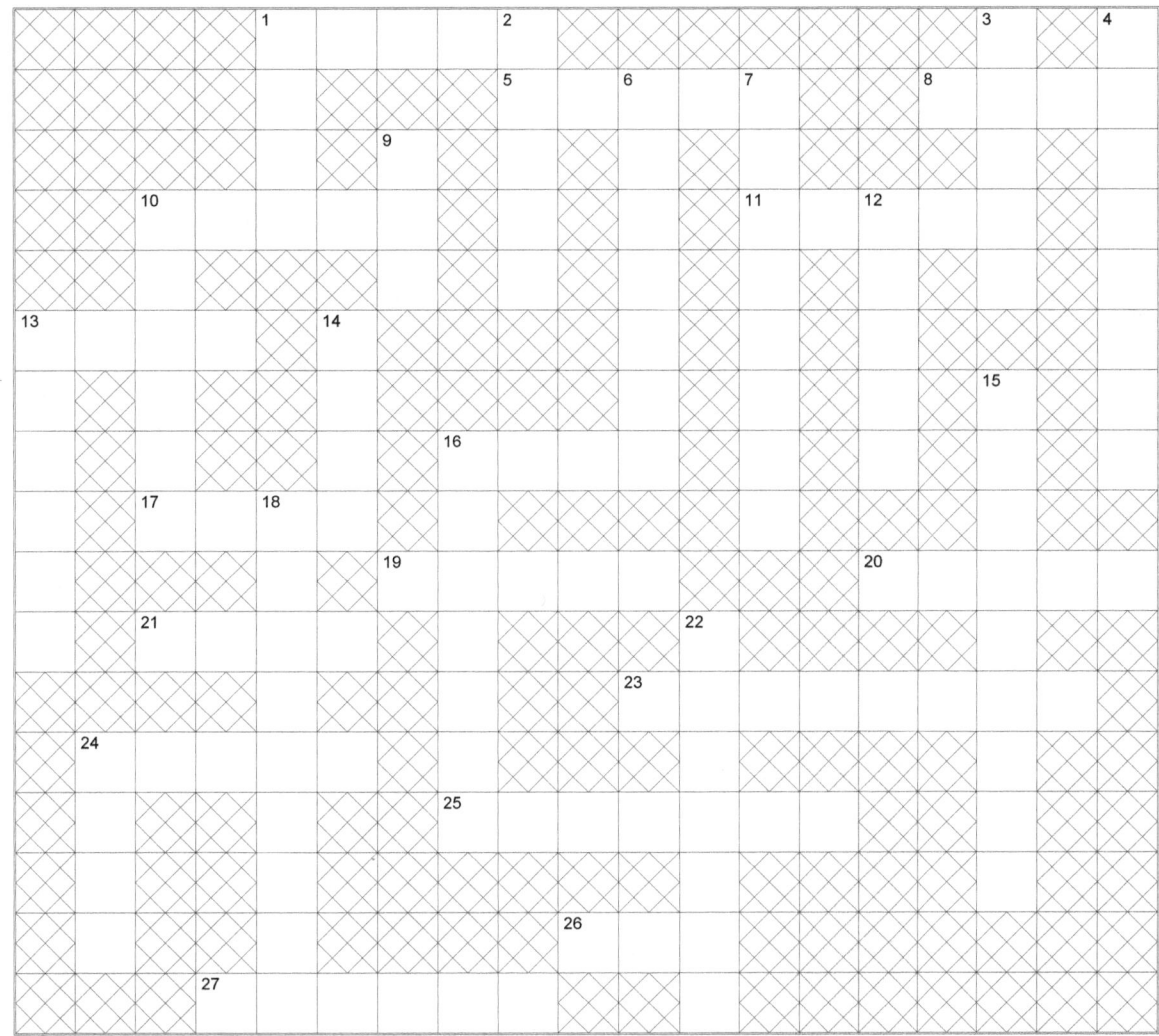

Across
1. James was hooked on these
5. '____ are really changing'
8. 'A man must have some____'
10. Handicapped trainer and friend to Alfred
11. Bully; gang leader
13. Alfred told his aunt a dog knocked him off a stone ____
16. Tried to recruit Alfred
17. How Alfred felt after his 2nd fight
19. Ex-fighter; teacher
20. Alfred forgot to tell the gang about it
21. 'You should have your own____, do what you want'
23. 'Nothing's____you, nothing's ever ____ you'
24. Alfred's best friend
25. Ex-fighter; Alfred's boss
26. The 'cut man'; assistant manager
27. Alfred's last name

Down
1. 'People will try to drag you____'
2. Epstein's establishment
3. Alfred's aunt
4. Practicing
6. ____ Square Garden
7. 'Everybody is ____'
9. Place to work out and practice boxing
10. He, Major & Sonny beat up Alfred
12. ____Belly; lacked self-discipline with food
13. He says to look for opportunities for the future
14. Place Alfred liked to run
15. Boxing manager
16. Author
18. The____
22. Relationship between Alfred and James
24. Alfred knocked him down while sparring

Contender Crossword 4 Answer Key

				¹D	R	U	²G	S					³P		⁴T
				O			⁵T	⁶I	⁷M	E	S		⁸F	E	A	R
				W		⁹G		O		A		S			O	A	
		¹⁰H	E	N	R	Y		R		D			¹¹M	¹²J	O	R
		O				M		E		I			E	E		L	I
¹³W	A	L	L		¹⁴P				S		B		L				
I		L			A				O		O		L	¹⁵D		N
L		I			R		¹⁶L	Y	N	N		D		Y		O	G
S		¹⁷S	¹⁸C	K			I				Y				N	
O			O		¹⁹S	P	O	O	N			²⁰A	L	A	R	M
N		²¹M	I	N	D				²²F					T		
			T			Y			²³P	R	O	M	I	S	E	D
		²⁴J	A	M	E	S		I				L			
		O				²⁵E	P	S	T	E	I	N		L	
		S		D						N				I	
		E		E			²⁶B	U	D				
			²⁷B	R	O	O	K	S			S		

Across
1. James was hooked on these
5. '____ are really changing'
8. 'A man must have some____'
10. Handicapped trainer and friend to Alfred
11. Bully; gang leader
13. Alfred told his aunt a dog knocked him off a stone ____
16. Tried to recruit Alfred
17. How Alfred felt after his 2nd fight
19. Ex-fighter; teacher
20. Alfred forgot to tell the gang about it
21. 'You should have your own____, do what you want'
23. 'Nothing's____you, nothing's ever ____ you'
24. Alfred's best friend
25. Ex-fighter; Alfred's boss
26. The 'cut man'; assistant manager
27. Alfred's last name

Down
1. 'People will try to drag you____'
2. Epstein's establishment
3. Alfred's aunt
4. Practicing
6. ____ Square Garden
7. 'Everybody is ____'
9. Place to work out and practice boxing
10. He, Major & Sonny beat up Alfred
12. ____Belly; lacked self-discipline with food
13. He says to look for opportunities for the future
14. Place Alfred liked to run
15. Boxing manager
16. Author
18. The____
22. Relationship between Alfred and James
24. Alfred knocked him down while sparring

Contender

WALL	TIMES	JOSE	FRIENDS	WILSON
LYNN	HOLLIS	MAJOR	JELLY	ALFRED
BROOKS	MIND	FREE SPACE	DONATELLI	PEARL
GRIFFIN	CONTENDER	CLUBHOUSE	ALARM	CLIMBING
SOMEBODY	GYM	PROMISED	BUD	MADISON

Contender

JAMES	TRAINING	DOWN	EPSTEIN	STORE
PARK	SICK	LIPSYTE	FEAR	SPOON
HENRY	MADISON	FREE SPACE	PROMISED	GYM
SOMEBODY	CLIMBING	ALARM	CLUBHOUSE	CONTENDER
GRIFFIN	PEARL	DONATELLI	DRUGS	MIND

Contender

PEARL	WILSON	DRUGS	HOLLIS	LYNN
EPSTEIN	WALL	FRIENDS	SOMEBODY	TRAINING
ALFRED	SICK	FREE SPACE	BUD	PROMISED
CLUBHOUSE	STORE	TIMES	MIND	JAMES
CLIMBING	GRIFFIN	DONATELLI	CONTENDER	HENRY

Contender

LIPSYTE	BROOKS	ALARM	GYM	MADISON
FEAR	JOSE	DOWN	MAJOR	PARK
SPOON	HENRY	FREE SPACE	DONATELLI	GRIFFIN
CLIMBING	JAMES	MIND	TIMES	STORE
CLUBHOUSE	PROMISED	BUD	JELLY	SICK

Contender

MIND	PEARL	CLUBHOUSE	DRUGS	JOSE
DOWN	DONATELLI	MADISON	SOMEBODY	HOLLIS
JELLY	PARK	FREE SPACE	PROMISED	LIPSYTE
SICK	WILSON	ALFRED	CLIMBING	GYM
JAMES	MAJOR	EPSTEIN	BROOKS	TRAINING

Contender

TIMES	STORE	FEAR	HENRY	GRIFFIN
WALL	FRIENDS	LYNN	CONTENDER	ALARM
BUD	TRAINING	FREE SPACE	EPSTEIN	MAJOR
JAMES	GYM	CLIMBING	ALFRED	WILSON
SICK	LIPSYTE	PROMISED	SPOON	PARK

Contender

STORE	CONTENDER	ALARM	CLUBHOUSE	FEAR
TIMES	SOMEBODY	PARK	JAMES	HENRY
JELLY	TRAINING	FREE SPACE	SPOON	MIND
MADISON	ALFRED	BROOKS	PROMISED	DONATELLI
SICK	BUD	MAJOR	CLIMBING	WALL

Contender

DOWN	JOSE	FRIENDS	DRUGS	LYNN
LIPSYTE	HOLLIS	WILSON	PEARL	GRIFFIN
GYM	WALL	FREE SPACE	MAJOR	BUD
SICK	DONATELLI	PROMISED	BROOKS	ALFRED
MADISON	MIND	SPOON	EPSTEIN	TRAINING

Contender

DRUGS	WALL	JAMES	SOMEBODY	PEARL
PROMISED	TRAINING	CONTENDER	MADISON	HOLLIS
SPOON	STORE	FREE SPACE	PARK	CLUBHOUSE
SICK	FEAR	ALARM	ALFRED	JOSE
WILSON	CLIMBING	GRIFFIN	BROOKS	MAJOR

Contender

FRIENDS	LYNN	LIPSYTE	MIND	TIMES
GYM	DOWN	EPSTEIN	HENRY	JELLY
BUD	MAJOR	FREE SPACE	GRIFFIN	CLIMBING
WILSON	JOSE	ALFRED	ALARM	FEAR
SICK	CLUBHOUSE	PARK	DONATELLI	STORE

Contender

HENRY	TRAINING	BUD	LYNN	GYM
FRIENDS	CLUBHOUSE	PEARL	MIND	JOSE
MADISON	DRUGS	FREE SPACE	LIPSYTE	TIMES
BROOKS	DOWN	ALFRED	ALARM	MAJOR
DONATELLI	CLIMBING	JAMES	JELLY	HOLLIS

Contender

GRIFFIN	EPSTEIN	SOMEBODY	SPOON	WALL
WILSON	SICK	STORE	CONTENDER	FEAR
PARK	HOLLIS	FREE SPACE	JAMES	CLIMBING
DONATELLI	MAJOR	ALARM	ALFRED	DOWN
BROOKS	TIMES	LIPSYTE	PROMISED	DRUGS

Contender

LYNN	BUD	SOMEBODY	SICK	ALARM
HOLLIS	WALL	MADISON	LIPSYTE	PEARL
MIND	ALFRED	FREE SPACE	SPOON	DOWN
CONTENDER	PROMISED	BROOKS	DONATELLI	CLUBHOUSE
TRAINING	GRIFFIN	FEAR	WILSON	MAJOR

Contender

TIMES	JOSE	DRUGS	GYM	JAMES
STORE	JELLY	CLIMBING	PARK	HENRY
EPSTEIN	MAJOR	FREE SPACE	FEAR	GRIFFIN
TRAINING	CLUBHOUSE	DONATELLI	BROOKS	PROMISED
CONTENDER	DOWN	SPOON	FRIENDS	ALFRED

Contender

HENRY	CLIMBING	ALFRED	TRAINING	JELLY
STORE	JOSE	EPSTEIN	SPOON	MIND
PEARL	ALARM	FREE SPACE	GYM	TIMES
PARK	MADISON	CONTENDER	GRIFFIN	JAMES
SOMEBODY	PROMISED	FEAR	DONATELLI	MAJOR

Contender

LYNN	FRIENDS	WILSON	DOWN	LIPSYTE
HOLLIS	DRUGS	BUD	CLUBHOUSE	SICK
BROOKS	MAJOR	FREE SPACE	FEAR	PROMISED
SOMEBODY	JAMES	GRIFFIN	CONTENDER	MADISON
PARK	TIMES	GYM	WALL	ALARM

Contender

SPOON	TIMES	STORE	WALL	CLIMBING
EPSTEIN	LIPSYTE	BROOKS	JELLY	CLUBHOUSE
GYM	MIND	FREE SPACE	MAJOR	HOLLIS
MADISON	HENRY	DONATELLI	DOWN	ALARM
PARK	FEAR	DRUGS	PROMISED	ALFRED

Contender

WILSON	PEARL	FRIENDS	JAMES	SOMEBODY
GRIFFIN	JOSE	CONTENDER	TRAINING	BUD
SICK	ALFRED	FREE SPACE	DRUGS	FEAR
PARK	ALARM	DOWN	DONATELLI	HENRY
MADISON	HOLLIS	MAJOR	LYNN	MIND

Contender

MADISON	ALFRED	CLIMBING	BUD	CONTENDER
TIMES	FRIENDS	SPOON	DRUGS	MAJOR
CLUBHOUSE	ALARM	FREE SPACE	MIND	HOLLIS
BROOKS	HENRY	GRIFFIN	PROMISED	JELLY
EPSTEIN	LYNN	LIPSYTE	DOWN	WILSON

Contender

SICK	GYM	STORE	DONATELLI	PEARL
SOMEBODY	JAMES	WALL	FEAR	TRAINING
PARK	WILSON	FREE SPACE	LIPSYTE	LYNN
EPSTEIN	JELLY	PROMISED	GRIFFIN	HENRY
BROOKS	HOLLIS	MIND	JOSE	ALARM

Contender

ALFRED	CLUBHOUSE	FEAR	CLIMBING	TRAINING
FRIENDS	ALARM	TIMES	BUD	DRUGS
MADISON	BROOKS	FREE SPACE	CONTENDER	PEARL
MIND	WALL	LYNN	WILSON	GYM
SOMEBODY	DONATELLI	SPOON	JOSE	HOLLIS

Contender

PARK	GRIFFIN	DOWN	EPSTEIN	PROMISED
SICK	HENRY	LIPSYTE	JAMES	JELLY
MAJOR	HOLLIS	FREE SPACE	SPOON	DONATELLI
SOMEBODY	GYM	WILSON	LYNN	WALL
MIND	PEARL	CONTENDER	STORE	BROOKS

Contender

SICK	DRUGS	SPOON	HENRY	LIPSYTE
WALL	FRIENDS	CONTENDER	DOWN	JAMES
CLUBHOUSE	JELLY	FREE SPACE	BUD	FEAR
JOSE	ALARM	PARK	PEARL	TRAINING
STORE	TIMES	ALFRED	MADISON	GYM

Contender

MIND	LYNN	DONATELLI	SOMEBODY	PROMISED
MAJOR	EPSTEIN	WILSON	CLIMBING	GRIFFIN
HOLLIS	GYM	FREE SPACE	ALFRED	TIMES
STORE	TRAINING	PEARL	PARK	ALARM
JOSE	FEAR	BUD	BROOKS	JELLY

Contender

DRUGS	MAJOR	BROOKS	STORE	HOLLIS
DOWN	CLUBHOUSE	SICK	GYM	FEAR
MIND	WILSON	FREE SPACE	JELLY	HENRY
TIMES	JAMES	WALL	LYNN	CONTENDER
SPOON	BUD	ALFRED	FRIENDS	PARK

Contender

JOSE	MADISON	ALARM	EPSTEIN	CLIMBING
LIPSYTE	PEARL	SOMEBODY	GRIFFIN	PROMISED
TRAINING	PARK	FREE SPACE	ALFRED	BUD
SPOON	CONTENDER	LYNN	WALL	JAMES
TIMES	HENRY	JELLY	DONATELLI	WILSON

Contender

WILSON	CONTENDER	BROOKS	PROMISED	DRUGS
WALL	JOSE	GRIFFIN	SOMEBODY	HENRY
STORE	SPOON	FREE SPACE	TRAINING	PARK
MADISON	ALARM	JAMES	FEAR	LIPSYTE
JELLY	HOLLIS	SICK	MIND	PEARL

Contender

CLUBHOUSE	MAJOR	BUD	CLIMBING	DONATELLI
EPSTEIN	ALFRED	TIMES	FRIENDS	DOWN
LYNN	PEARL	FREE SPACE	SICK	HOLLIS
JELLY	LIPSYTE	FEAR	JAMES	ALARM
MADISON	PARK	TRAINING	GYM	SPOON

Contender

GYM	ALFRED	CLIMBING	MAJOR	BUD
PARK	CLUBHOUSE	EPSTEIN	DRUGS	PROMISED
WALL	STORE	FREE SPACE	DOWN	SICK
LYNN	HENRY	TIMES	JOSE	BROOKS
GRIFFIN	FEAR	JELLY	LIPSYTE	HOLLIS

Contender

SPOON	FRIENDS	TRAINING	DONATELLI	MIND
PEARL	WILSON	ALARM	SOMEBODY	MADISON
CONTENDER	HOLLIS	FREE SPACE	JELLY	FEAR
GRIFFIN	BROOKS	JOSE	TIMES	HENRY
LYNN	SICK	DOWN	JAMES	STORE

Contender

ALFRED	GRIFFIN	HOLLIS	JOSE	MADISON
JAMES	LIPSYTE	DRUGS	SPOON	SICK
CLIMBING	PEARL	FREE SPACE	SOMEBODY	PARK
HENRY	TIMES	JELLY	TRAINING	PROMISED
BROOKS	DOWN	MIND	CLUBHOUSE	WILSON

Contender

WALL	FRIENDS	BUD	FEAR	LYNN
DONATELLI	EPSTEIN	STORE	CONTENDER	MAJOR
GYM	WILSON	FREE SPACE	MIND	DOWN
BROOKS	PROMISED	TRAINING	JELLY	TIMES
HENRY	PARK	SOMEBODY	ALARM	PEARL

Contender Vocabulary Word List

No.	Word	Clue/Definition
1.	ADDICT	Dependent on a habit-forming substance
2.	AMATEUR	A person who does an activity as a hobby instead of for pay
3.	CHAUFFEUR	One employed to drive an automobile
4.	CONCENTRATED	Diligently thought about; focused
5.	CORRIDOR	Hallway
6.	CUFFING	Hitting with an open hand
7.	DIGNIFIED	With reserve; showing decorum; with dignity
8.	ELEGANTLY	In a refined manner; classically beautifully
9.	EMBLEM	Insignia; symbolic badge or design
10.	ENCASED	Enclosed
11.	FUNKY	Earthy and uncomplicated; natural
12.	HYPNOTIZED	In a trance
13.	IMPATIENTLY	Restlessly; anxiously
14.	LAPSED	Passed; expired
15.	LISTLESSNESS	Hum-drum; lifelessness; boredom
16.	LURCHED	Rolled or pitched suddenly or erratically
17.	MINGLED	Mixed
18.	MUTED	Muffled; sound made soft by distance or interference
19.	PARALYZING	Making unable to move or act
20.	PEAL	A loud burst of noise
21.	PERPETUAL	Continuing without interruption
22.	PRELIMINARY	That which goes before or prepares
23.	PUMMELING	Beating with fists
24.	PURSUIT	Activity engage in regularly; an endeavor
25.	SERENE	Calm; unruffled
26.	SHRUGGED	Moved shoulders up and down as a gesture of doubt or indifference
27.	SILHOUETTED	Seen as a dark outline against a light background
28.	SULLEN	Gloomy
29.	TENEMENT	A rundown, low-rent apartment building
30.	VAGUELY	Indistinctly; unclearly
31.	VAULTED	Jumped
32.	VEERED	Turned towards one side

Contender Vocabulary Fill In The Blanks 1

1. Hum-drum; lifelessness; boredom
2. Insignia; symbolic badge or design
3. In a refined manner; classically beautifully
4. Restlessly; anxiously
5. A person who does an activity as a hobby instead of for pay
6. A rundown, low-rent apartment building
7. Continuing without interruption
8. Diligently thought about; focused
9. Mixed
10. Hallway
11. Gloomy
12. Enclosed
13. Muffled; sound made soft by distance or interference
14. Turned towards one side
15. That which goes before or prepares
16. Making unable to move or act
17. Moved shoulders up and down as a gesture of doubt or indifference
18. Earthy and uncomplicated; natural
19. Dependent on a habit-forming substance
20. Calm; unruffled

Contender Vocabulary Fill In The Blanks 1 Answer Key

LISTLESSNESS	1. Hum-drum; lifelessness; boredom
EMBLEM	2. Insignia; symbolic badge or design
ELEGANTLY	3. In a refined manner; classically beautifully
IMPATIENTLY	4. Restlessly; anxiously
AMATEUR	5. A person who does an activity as a hobby instead of for pay
TENEMENT	6. A rundown, low-rent apartment building
PERPETUAL	7. Continuing without interruption
CONCENTRATED	8. Diligently thought about; focused
MINGLED	9. Mixed
CORRIDOR	10. Hallway
SULLEN	11. Gloomy
ENCASED	12. Enclosed
MUTED	13. Muffled; sound made soft by distance or interference
VEERED	14. Turned towards one side
PRELIMINARY	15. That which goes before or prepares
PARALYZING	16. Making unable to move or act
SHRUGGED	17. Moved shoulders up and down as a gesture of doubt or indifference
FUNKY	18. Earthy and uncomplicated; natural
ADDICT	19. Dependent on a habit-forming substance
SERENE	20. Calm; unruffled

Contender Vocabulary Fill In The Blanks 2

1. Enclosed
2. Gloomy
3. With reserve; showing decorum; with dignity
4. Diligently thought about; focused
5. Turned towards one side
6. Hitting with an open hand
7. Activity engage in regularly; an endeavor
8. Hallway
9. Muffled; sound made soft by distance or interference
10. Moved shoulders up and down as a gesture of doubt or indifference
11. Indistinctly; unclearly
12. Dependent on a habit-forming substance
13. Rolled or pitched suddenly or erratically
14. Mixed
15. Earthy and uncomplicated; natural
16. A person who does an activity as a hobby instead of for pay
17. In a trance
18. Beating with fists
19. Hum-drum; lifelessness; boredom
20. Restlessly; anxiously

Contender Vocabulary Fill In The Blanks 2 Answer Key

ENCASED	1. Enclosed
SULLEN	2. Gloomy
DIGNIFIED	3. With reserve; showing decorum; with dignity
CONCENTRATED	4. Diligently thought about; focused
VEERED	5. Turned towards one side
CUFFING	6. Hitting with an open hand
PURSUIT	7. Activity engage in regularly; an endeavor
CORRIDOR	8. Hallway
MUTED	9. Muffled; sound made soft by distance or interference
SHRUGGED	10. Moved shoulders up and down as a gesture of doubt or indifference
VAGUELY	11. Indistinctly; unclearly
ADDICT	12. Dependent on a habit-forming substance
LURCHED	13. Rolled or pitched suddenly or erratically
MINGLED	14. Mixed
FUNKY	15. Earthy and uncomplicated; natural
AMATEUR	16. A person who does an activity as a hobby instead of for pay
HYPNOTIZED	17. In a trance
PUMMELING	18. Beating with fists
LISTLESSNESS	19. Hum-drum; lifelessness; boredom
IMPATIENTLY	20. Restlessly; anxiously

Contender Vocabulary Fill In The Blanks 3

1. Diligently thought about; focused
2. Turned towards one side
3. Rolled or pitched suddenly or erratically
4. Jumped
5. Making unable to move or act
6. Continuing without interruption
7. Hum-drum; lifelessness; boredom
8. Mixed
9. Moved shoulders up and down as a gesture of doubt or indifference
10. Indistinctly; unclearly
11. Seen as a dark outline against a light background
12. Enclosed
13. Dependent on a habit-forming substance
14. In a trance
15. Activity engage in regularly; an endeavor
16. Restlessly; anxiously
17. Passed; expired
18. Calm; unruffled
19. Insignia; symbolic badge or design
20. A loud burst of noise

Contender Vocabulary Fill In The Blanks 3 Answer Key

CONCENTRATED	1. Diligently thought about; focused
VEERED	2. Turned towards one side
LURCHED	3. Rolled or pitched suddenly or erratically
VAULTED	4. Jumped
PARALYZING	5. Making unable to move or act
PERPETUAL	6. Continuing without interruption
LISTLESSNESS	7. Hum-drum; lifelessness; boredom
MINGLED	8. Mixed
SHRUGGED	9. Moved shoulders up and down as a gesture of doubt or indifference
VAGUELY	10. Indistinctly; unclearly
SILHOUETTED	11. Seen as a dark outline against a light background
ENCASED	12. Enclosed
ADDICT	13. Dependent on a habit-forming substance
HYPNOTIZED	14. In a trance
PURSUIT	15. Activity engage in regularly; an endeavor
IMPATIENTLY	16. Restlessly; anxiously
LAPSED	17. Passed; expired
SERENE	18. Calm; unruffled
EMBLEM	19. Insignia; symbolic badge or design
PEAL	20. A loud burst of noise

Contender Vocabulary Fill In The Blanks 4

1. A person who does an activity as a hobby instead of for pay
2. Diligently thought about; focused
3. Rolled or pitched suddenly or erratically
4. Moved shoulders up and down as a gesture of doubt or indifference
5. Beating with fists
6. Turned towards one side
7. In a refined manner; classically beautifully
8. Hallway
9. Mixed
10. Dependent on a habit-forming substance
11. One employed to drive an automobile
12. A rundown, low-rent apartment building
13. That which goes before or prepares
14. Seen as a dark outline against a light background
15. Hitting with an open hand
16. In a trance
17. Continuing without interruption
18. Hum-drum; lifelessness; boredom
19. Making unable to move or act
20. Gloomy

Contender Vocabulary Fill In The Blanks 4 Answer Key

AMATEUR		1. A person who does an activity as a hobby instead of for pay
CONCENTRATED		2. Diligently thought about; focused
LURCHED		3. Rolled or pitched suddenly or erratically
SHRUGGED		4. Moved shoulders up and down as a gesture of doubt or indifference
PUMMELING		5. Beating with fists
VEERED		6. Turned towards one side
ELEGANTLY		7. In a refined manner; classically beautifully
CORRIDOR		8. Hallway
MINGLED		9. Mixed
ADDICT		10. Dependent on a habit-forming substance
CHAUFFEUR		11. One employed to drive an automobile
TENEMENT		12. A rundown, low-rent apartment building
PRELIMINARY		13. That which goes before or prepares
SILHOUETTED		14. Seen as a dark outline against a light background
CUFFING		15. Hitting with an open hand
HYPNOTIZED		16. In a trance
PERPETUAL		17. Continuing without interruption
LISTLESSNESS		18. Hum-drum; lifelessness; boredom
PARALYZING		19. Making unable to move or act
SULLEN		20. Gloomy

Contender Vocabulary Matching 1

___ 1. LAPSED
___ 2. ELEGANTLY
___ 3. CONCENTRATED
___ 4. PUMMELING
___ 5. VEERED
___ 6. SILHOUETTED
___ 7. PRELIMINARY
___ 8. MINGLED
___ 9. TENEMENT
___10. HYPNOTIZED
___11. SHRUGGED
___12. PERPETUAL
___13. LISTLESSNESS
___14. ADDICT
___15. AMATEUR
___16. PARALYZING
___17. LURCHED
___18. CHAUFFEUR
___19. CORRIDOR
___20. PEAL
___21. MUTED
___22. PURSUIT
___23. SULLEN
___24. EMBLEM
___25. FUNKY

A. Mixed
B. That which goes before or prepares
C. Turned towards one side
D. Passed; expired
E. A person who does an activity as a hobby instead of for pay
F. In a refined manner; classically beautifully
G. Seen as a dark outline against a light background
H. Activity engage in regularly; an endeavor
I. Hum-drum; lifelessness; boredom
J. Diligently thought about; focused
K. Making unable to move or act
L. Rolled or pitched suddenly or erratically
M. One employed to drive an automobile
N. A rundown, low-rent apartment building
O. A loud burst of noise
P. Dependent on a habit-forming substance
Q. Insignia; symbolic badge or design
R. Earthy and uncomplicated; natural
S. Continuing without interruption
T. Hallway
U. Gloomy
V. Muffled; sound made soft by distance or interference
W. In a trance
X. Moved shoulders up and down as a gesture of doubt or indifference
Y. Beating with fists

Contender Vocabulary Matching 1 Answer Key

- D - 1. LAPSED
- F - 2. ELEGANTLY
- J - 3. CONCENTRATED
- Y - 4. PUMMELING
- C - 5. VEERED
- G - 6. SILHOUETTED
- B - 7. PRELIMINARY
- A - 8. MINGLED
- N - 9. TENEMENT
- W - 10. HYPNOTIZED
- X - 11. SHRUGGED
- S - 12. PERPETUAL
- I - 13. LISTLESSNESS
- P - 14. ADDICT
- E - 15. AMATEUR
- K - 16. PARALYZING
- L - 17. LURCHED
- M - 18. CHAUFFEUR
- T - 19. CORRIDOR
- O - 20. PEAL
- V - 21. MUTED
- H - 22. PURSUIT
- U - 23. SULLEN
- Q - 24. EMBLEM
- R - 25. FUNKY

A. Mixed
B. That which goes before or prepares
C. Turned towards one side
D. Passed; expired
E. A person who does an activity as a hobby instead of for pay
F. In a refined manner; classically beautifully
G. Seen as a dark outline against a light background
H. Activity engage in regularly; an endeavor
I. Hum-drum; lifelessness; boredom
J. Diligently thought about; focused
K. Making unable to move or act
L. Rolled or pitched suddenly or erratically
M. One employed to drive an automobile
N. A rundown, low-rent apartment building
O. A loud burst of noise
P. Dependent on a habit-forming substance
Q. Insignia; symbolic badge or design
R. Earthy and uncomplicated; natural
S. Continuing without interruption
T. Hallway
U. Gloomy
V. Muffled; sound made soft by distance or interference
W. In a trance
X. Moved shoulders up and down as a gesture of doubt or indifference
Y. Beating with fists

Contender Vocabulary Matching 2

___ 1. MUTED
___ 2. HYPNOTIZED
___ 3. SULLEN
___ 4. AMATEUR
___ 5. CORRIDOR
___ 6. VAULTED
___ 7. PUMMELING
___ 8. PEAL
___ 9. SHRUGGED
___ 10. ELEGANTLY
___ 11. PRELIMINARY
___ 12. CONCENTRATED
___ 13. PURSUIT
___ 14. EMBLEM
___ 15. TENEMENT
___ 16. DIGNIFIED
___ 17. LURCHED
___ 18. SERENE
___ 19. CUFFING
___ 20. IMPATIENTLY
___ 21. VAGUELY
___ 22. FUNKY
___ 23. MINGLED
___ 24. PARALYZING
___ 25. CHAUFFEUR

A. In a refined manner; classically beautifully
B. Calm; unruffled
C. Making unable to move or act
D. With reserve; showing decorum; with dignity
E. Activity engage in regularly; an endeavor
F. Rolled or pitched suddenly or erratically
G. Mixed
H. One employed to drive an automobile
I. A rundown, low-rent apartment building
J. A loud burst of noise
K. Hallway
L. That which goes before or prepares
M. Gloomy
N. Hitting with an open hand
O. Jumped
P. Restlessly; anxiously
Q. Indistinctly; unclearly
R. In a trance
S. Diligently thought about; focused
T. Insignia; symbolic badge or design
U. Beating with fists
V. Muffled; sound made soft by distance or interference
W. Earthy and uncomplicated; natural
X. Moved shoulders up and down as a gesture of doubt or indifference
Y. A person who does an activity as a hobby instead of for pay

Contender Vocabulary Matching 2 Answer Key

V - 1. MUTED	A.	In a refined manner; classically beautifully
R - 2. HYPNOTIZED	B.	Calm; unruffled
M - 3. SULLEN	C.	Making unable to move or act
Y - 4. AMATEUR	D.	With reserve; showing decorum; with dignity
K - 5. CORRIDOR	E.	Activity engage in regularly; an endeavor
O - 6. VAULTED	F.	Rolled or pitched suddenly or erratically
U - 7. PUMMELING	G.	Mixed
J - 8. PEAL	H.	One employed to drive an automobile
X - 9. SHRUGGED	I.	A rundown, low-rent apartment building
A - 10. ELEGANTLY	J.	A loud burst of noise
L - 11. PRELIMINARY	K.	Hallway
S - 12. CONCENTRATED	L.	That which goes before or prepares
E - 13. PURSUIT	M.	Gloomy
T - 14. EMBLEM	N.	Hitting with an open hand
I - 15. TENEMENT	O.	Jumped
D - 16. DIGNIFIED	P.	Restlessly; anxiously
F - 17. LURCHED	Q.	Indistinctly; unclearly
B - 18. SERENE	R.	In a trance
N - 19. CUFFING	S.	Diligently thought about; focused
P - 20. IMPATIENTLY	T.	Insignia; symbolic badge or design
Q - 21. VAGUELY	U.	Beating with fists
W - 22. FUNKY	V.	Muffled; sound made soft by distance or interference
G - 23. MINGLED	W.	Earthy and uncomplicated; natural
C - 24. PARALYZING	X.	Moved shoulders up and down as a gesture of doubt or indifference
H - 25. CHAUFFEUR	Y.	A person who does an activity as a hobby instead of for pay

Contender Vocabulary Matching 3

___ 1. LURCHED   A. Calm; unruffled
___ 2. PERPETUAL   B. Mixed
___ 3. CHAUFFEUR   C. Moved shoulders up and down as a gesture of doubt or indifference
___ 4. PUMMELING   D. A loud burst of noise
___ 5. MINGLED   E. Jumped
___ 6. SULLEN   F. That which goes before or prepares
___ 7. AMATEUR   G. Muffled; sound made soft by distance or interference
___ 8. PEAL   H. In a trance
___ 9. CUFFING   I. A person who does an activity as a hobby instead of for pay
___ 10. MUTED   J. One employed to drive an automobile
___ 11. VEERED   K. A rundown, low-rent apartment building
___ 12. PRELIMINARY   L. Continuing without interruption
___ 13. FUNKY   M. Beating with fists
___ 14. VAGUELY   N. Earthy and uncomplicated; natural
___ 15. SERENE   O. Hitting with an open hand
___ 16. CONCENTRATED P. Dependent on a habit-forming substance
___ 17. TENEMENT   Q. Activity engage in regularly; an endeavor
___ 18. ADDICT   R. Insignia; symbolic badge or design
___ 19. SHRUGGED   S. Indistinctly; unclearly
___ 20. VAULTED   T. Rolled or pitched suddenly or erratically
___ 21. PURSUIT   U. With reserve; showing decorum; with dignity
___ 22. DIGNIFIED   V. Turned towards one side
___ 23. EMBLEM   W. Enclosed
___ 24. ENCASED   X. Diligently thought about; focused
___ 25. HYPNOTIZED   Y. Gloomy

Contender Vocabulary Matching 3 Answer Key

T - 1. LURCHED	A.	Calm; unruffled
L - 2. PERPETUAL	B.	Mixed
J - 3. CHAUFFEUR	C.	Moved shoulders up and down as a gesture of doubt or indifference
M - 4. PUMMELING	D.	A loud burst of noise
B - 5. MINGLED	E.	Jumped
Y - 6. SULLEN	F.	That which goes before or prepares
I - 7. AMATEUR	G.	Muffled; sound made soft by distance or interference
D - 8. PEAL	H.	In a trance
O - 9. CUFFING	I.	A person who does an activity as a hobby instead of for pay
G - 10. MUTED	J.	One employed to drive an automobile
V - 11. VEERED	K.	A rundown, low-rent apartment building
F - 12. PRELIMINARY	L.	Continuing without interruption
N - 13. FUNKY	M.	Beating with fists
S - 14. VAGUELY	N.	Earthy and uncomplicated; natural
A - 15. SERENE	O.	Hitting with an open hand
X - 16. CONCENTRATED	P.	Dependent on a habit-forming substance
K - 17. TENEMENT	Q.	Activity engage in regularly; an endeavor
P - 18. ADDICT	R.	Insignia; symbolic badge or design
C - 19. SHRUGGED	S.	Indistinctly; unclearly
E - 20. VAULTED	T.	Rolled or pitched suddenly or erratically
Q - 21. PURSUIT	U.	With reserve; showing decorum; with dignity
U - 22. DIGNIFIED	V.	Turned towards one side
R - 23. EMBLEM	W.	Enclosed
W - 24. ENCASED	X.	Diligently thought about; focused
H - 25. HYPNOTIZED	Y.	Gloomy

Contender Vocabulary Matching 4

___ 1. FUNKY   A. A loud burst of noise
___ 2. MINGLED   B. That which goes before or prepares
___ 3. VEERED   C. Gloomy
___ 4. CONCENTRATED D. Passed; expired
___ 5. LISTLESSNESS E. Restlessly; anxiously
___ 6. TENEMENT   F. Hitting with an open hand
___ 7. LAPSED   G. Continuing without interruption
___ 8. PURSUIT   H. Turned towards one side
___ 9. PERPETUAL   I. Insignia; symbolic badge or design
___10. PUMMELING   J. Indistinctly; unclearly
___11. LURCHED   K. Dependent on a habit-forming substance
___12. SULLEN   L. Beating with fists
___13. PEAL   M. Rolled or pitched suddenly or erratically
___14. DIGNIFIED   N. Muffled; sound made soft by distance or interference
___15. VAULTED   O. Mixed
___16. CORRIDOR   P. Calm; unruffled
___17. IMPATIENTLY   Q. With reserve; showing decorum; with dignity
___18. CUFFING   R. Hum-drum; lifelessness; boredom
___19. VAGUELY   S. Jumped
___20. ADDICT   T. Hallway
___21. ENCASED   U. Enclosed
___22. EMBLEM   V. Activity engage in regularly; an endeavor
___23. PRELIMINARY   W. Diligently thought about; focused
___24. SERENE   X. A rundown, low-rent apartment building
___25. MUTED   Y. Earthy and uncomplicated; natural

Contender Vocabulary Matching 4 Answer Key

Y - 1.	FUNKY	A. A loud burst of noise
O - 2.	MINGLED	B. That which goes before or prepares
H - 3.	VEERED	C. Gloomy
W - 4.	CONCENTRATED	D. Passed; expired
R - 5.	LISTLESSNESS	E. Restlessly; anxiously
X - 6.	TENEMENT	F. Hitting with an open hand
D - 7.	LAPSED	G. Continuing without interruption
V - 8.	PURSUIT	H. Turned towards one side
G - 9.	PERPETUAL	I. Insignia; symbolic badge or design
L - 10.	PUMMELING	J. Indistinctly; unclearly
M - 11.	LURCHED	K. Dependent on a habit-forming substance
C - 12.	SULLEN	L. Beating with fists
A - 13.	PEAL	M. Rolled or pitched suddenly or erratically
Q - 14.	DIGNIFIED	N. Muffled; sound made soft by distance or interference
S - 15.	VAULTED	O. Mixed
T - 16.	CORRIDOR	P. Calm; unruffled
E - 17.	IMPATIENTLY	Q. With reserve; showing decorum; with dignity
F - 18.	CUFFING	R. Hum-drum; lifelessness; boredom
J - 19.	VAGUELY	S. Jumped
K - 20.	ADDICT	T. Hallway
U - 21.	ENCASED	U. Enclosed
I - 22.	EMBLEM	V. Activity engage in regularly; an endeavor
B - 23.	PRELIMINARY	W. Diligently thought about; focused
P - 24.	SERENE	X. A rundown, low-rent apartment building
N - 25.	MUTED	Y. Earthy and uncomplicated; natural

Contender Vocabulary Magic Squares 1

Match the definition with the vocabulary word. Put your answers in the magic squares below. When your answers are correct, all columns and rows will add to the same number.

A. SULLEN
B. ADDICT
C. HYPNOTIZED
D. EMBLEM
E. PUMMELING
F. PEAL
G. CHAUFFEUR
H. AMATEUR
I. PURSUIT
J. CORRIDOR
K. DIGNIFIED
L. LAPSED
M. ELEGANTLY
N. VAGUELY
O. ENCASED
P. SHRUGGED

1. Dependent on a habit-forming substance
2. One employed to drive an automobile
3. With reserve; showing decorum; with dignity
4. Indistinctly; unclearly
5. In a refined manner; classically beautifully
6. Passed; expired
7. A person who does an activity as a hobby instead of for pay
8. Gloomy
9. Moved shoulders up and down as a gesture of doubt or indifference
10. Activity engage in regularly; an endeavor
11. Beating with fists
12. Insignia; symbolic badge or design
13. In a trance
14. A loud burst of noise
15. Hallway
16. Enclosed

A=	B=	C=	D=
E=	F=	G=	H=
I=	J=	K=	L=
M=	N=	O=	P=

Contender Vocabulary Magic Squares 1 Answer Key

Match the definition with the vocabulary word. Put your answers in the magic squares below. When your answers are correct, all columns and rows will add to the same number.

A. SULLEN
B. ADDICT
C. HYPNOTIZED
D. EMBLEM
E. PUMMELING
F. PEAL
G. CHAUFFEUR
H. AMATEUR
I. PURSUIT
J. CORRIDOR
K. DIGNIFIED
L. LAPSED
M. ELEGANTLY
N. VAGUELY
O. ENCASED
P. SHRUGGED

1. Dependent on a habit-forming substance
2. One employed to drive an automobile
3. With reserve; showing decorum; with dignity
4. Indistinctly; unclearly
5. In a refined manner; classically beautifully
6. Passed; expired
7. A person who does an activity as a hobby instead of for pay
8. Gloomy
9. Moved shoulders up and down as a gesture of doubt or indifference
10. Activity engage in regularly; an endeavor
11. Beating with fists
12. Insignia; symbolic badge or design
13. In a trance
14. A loud burst of noise
15. Hallway
16. Enclosed

A=8	B=1	C=13	D=12
E=11	F=14	G=2	H=7
I=10	J=15	K=3	L=6
M=5	N=4	O=16	P=9

Contender Vocabulary Magic Squares 2

Match the definition with the vocabulary word. Put your answers in the magic squares below. When your answers are correct, all columns and rows will add to the same number.

A. PEAL
B. VAGUELY
C. VAULTED
D. AMATEUR
E. SILHOUETTED
F. CONCENTRATED
G. HYPNOTIZED
H. ELEGANTLY
I. CUFFING
J. CORRIDOR
K. TENEMENT
L. EMBLEM
M. VEERED
N. CHAUFFEUR
O. PRELIMINARY
P. PUMMELING

1. In a refined manner; classically beautifully
2. Turned towards one side
3. Indistinctly; unclearly
4. A rundown, low-rent apartment building
5. Hallway
6. Jumped
7. Beating with fists
8. Seen as a dark outline against a light background
9. That which goes before or prepares
10. Diligently thought about; focused
11. Hitting with an open hand
12. A person who does an activity as a hobby instead of for pay
13. A loud burst of noise
14. Insignia; symbolic badge or design
15. In a trance
16. One employed to drive an automobile

A= 13	B= 3	C= 6	D= 12
E= 8	F= 10	G= 15	H= 1
I= 11	J= 5	K= 4	L= 14
M= 2	N= 16	O= 9	P= 7

Contender Vocabulary Magic Squares 2 Answer Key

Match the definition with the vocabulary word. Put your answers in the magic squares below. When your answers are correct, all columns and rows will add to the same number.

A. PEAL
B. VAGUELY
C. VAULTED
D. AMATEUR
E. SILHOUETTED
F. CONCENTRATED
G. HYPNOTIZED
H. ELEGANTLY
I. CUFFING
J. CORRIDOR
K. TENEMENT
L. EMBLEM
M. VEERED
N. CHAUFFEUR
O. PRELIMINARY
P. PUMMELING

1. In a refined manner; classically beautifully
2. Turned towards one side
3. Indistinctly; unclearly
4. A rundown, low-rent apartment building
5. Hallway
6. Jumped
7. Beating with fists
8. Seen as a dark outline against a light background
9. That which goes before or prepares
10. Diligently thought about; focused
11. Hitting with an open hand
12. A person who does an activity as a hobby instead of for pay
13. A loud burst of noise
14. Insignia; symbolic badge or design
15. In a trance
16. One employed to drive an automobile

A=13	B=3	C=6	D=12
E=8	F=10	G=15	H=1
I=11	J=5	K=4	L=14
M=2	N=16	O=9	P=7

Contender Vocabulary Magic Squares 3

Match the definition with the vocabulary word. Put your answers in the magic squares below. When your answers are correct, all columns and rows will add to the same number.

A. CHAUFFEUR
B. DIGNIFIED
C. LURCHED
D. EMBLEM
E. ENCASED
F. FUNKY
G. PEAL
H. MINGLED
I. SERENE
J. PURSUIT
K. HYPNOTIZED
L. LISTLESSNESS
M. PERPETUAL
N. ADDICT
O. VEERED
P. VAGUELY

1. Rolled or pitched suddenly or erratically
2. Activity engage in regularly; an endeavor
3. Earthy and uncomplicated; natural
4. Turned towards one side
5. Indistinctly; unclearly
6. Enclosed
7. Calm; unruffled
8. Insignia; symbolic badge or design
9. Continuing without interruption
10. Mixed
11. Hum-drum; lifelessness; boredom
12. One employed to drive an automobile
13. With reserve; showing decorum; with dignity
14. In a trance
15. A loud burst of noise
16. Dependent on a habit-forming substance

A=	B=	C=	D=
E=	F=	G=	H=
I=	J=	K=	L=
M=	N=	O=	P=

Contender Vocabulary Magic Squares 3 Answer Key

Match the definition with the vocabulary word. Put your answers in the magic squares below. When your answers are correct, all columns and rows will add to the same number.

A. CHAUFFEUR
B. DIGNIFIED
C. LURCHED
D. EMBLEM
E. ENCASED
F. FUNKY
G. PEAL
H. MINGLED
I. SERENE
J. PURSUIT
K. HYPNOTIZED
L. LISTLESSNESS
M. PERPETUAL
N. ADDICT
O. VEERED
P. VAGUELY

1. Rolled or pitched suddenly or erratically
2. Activity engage in regularly; an endeavor
3. Earthy and uncomplicated; natural
4. Turned towards one side
5. Indistinctly; unclearly
6. Enclosed
7. Calm; unruffled
8. Insignia; symbolic badge or design
9. Continuing without interruption
10. Mixed
11. Hum-drum; lifelessness; boredom
12. One employed to drive an automobile
13. With reserve; showing decorum; with dignity
14. In a trance
15. A loud burst of noise
16. Dependent on a habit-forming substance

A=12	B=13	C=1	D=8
E=6	F=3	G=15	H=10
I=7	J=2	K=14	L=11
M=9	N=16	O=4	P=5

Contender Vocabulary Magic Squares 4

Match the definition with the vocabulary word. Put your answers in the magic squares below. When your answers are correct, all columns and rows will add to the same number.

A. MINGLED
B. CHAUFFEUR
C. PURSUIT
D. SILHOUETTED
E. PARALYZING
F. IMPATIENTLY
G. AMATEUR
H. DIGNIFIED
I. EMBLEM
J. LURCHED
K. ENCASED
L. ADDICT
M. PEAL
N. LAPSED
O. SULLEN
P. HYPNOTIZED

1. Restlessly; anxiously
2. Insignia; symbolic badge or design
3. Gloomy
4. Seen as a dark outline against a light background
5. A loud burst of noise
6. One employed to drive an automobile
7. With reserve; showing decorum; with dignity
8. Enclosed
9. Activity engage in regularly; an endeavor
10. In a trance
11. Rolled or pitched suddenly or erratically
12. Making unable to move or act
13. Dependent on a habit-forming substance
14. A person who does an activity as a hobby instead of for pay
15. Mixed
16. Passed; expired

A=	B=	C=	D=
E=	F=	G=	H=
I=	J=	K=	L=
M=	N=	O=	P=

Contender Vocabulary Magic Squares 4 Answer Key

Match the definition with the vocabulary word. Put your answers in the magic squares below. When your answers are correct, all columns and rows will add to the same number.

A. MINGLED
B. CHAUFFEUR
C. PURSUIT
D. SILHOUETTED
E. PARALYZING
F. IMPATIENTLY
G. AMATEUR
H. DIGNIFIED
I. EMBLEM
J. LURCHED
K. ENCASED
L. ADDICT
M. PEAL
N. LAPSED
O. SULLEN
P. HYPNOTIZED

1. Restlessly; anxiously
2. Insignia; symbolic badge or design
3. Gloomy
4. Seen as a dark outline against a light background
5. A loud burst of noise
6. One employed to drive an automobile
7. With reserve; showing decorum; with dignity
8. Enclosed
9. Activity engage in regularly; an endeavor
10. In a trance
11. Rolled or pitched suddenly or erratically
12. Making unable to move or act
13. Dependent on a habit-forming substance
14. A person who does an activity as a hobby instead of for pay
15. Mixed
16. Passed; expired

A=15	B=6	C=9	D=4
E=12	F=1	G=14	H=7
I=2	J=11	K=8	L=13
M=5	N=16	O=3	P=10

Contender Vocabulary Word Search 1

Words are placed backwards, forward, diagonally, up and down. Clues listed below can help you find the words. Circle the hidden vocabulary words in the maze.

P	R	E	L	I	M	I	N	A	R	Y	C	H	A	U	F	F	E	U	R
C	I	M	P	A	T	I	E	N	T	L	Y	Y	Q	D	S	R	L	M	Q
O	M	R	Y	N	F	C	T	D	B	N	Q	P	X	C	S	W	D	H	P
N	P	A	R	A	L	Y	Z	I	N	G	T	N	E	M	E	N	E	T	W
C	P	V	Z	R	L	Y	X	R	B	D	L	O	G	S	N	K	T	S	P
E	Q	G	T	Q	C	M	Y	Q	X	B	C	T	W	S	S	R	T	Y	Q
N	L	D	H	V	D	P	G	C	D	C	Y	I	P	K	S	V	E	Z	H
T	L	G	V	S	T	I	U	F	W	X	D	Z	B	P	E	Z	U	B	Z
R	A	D	V	X	Z	F	G	M	X	Z	D	E	G	W	L	Q	O	B	D
A	U	E	L	A	G	T	P	N	M	Q	G	D	P	S	T	X	H	F	G
T	T	H	J	G	G	N	F	K	I	E	Q	P	B	H	S	X	L	S	F
E	E	C	J	T	P	U	J	N	W	F	L	T	W	R	I	F	I	J	G
D	P	R	Q	E	R	V	E	Z	C	M	I	I	J	U	L	L	S	V	M
S	R	U	A	C	Z	V	R	L	E	C	P	E	N	G	N	V	N	I	K
R	E	L	E	G	A	N	T	L	Y	G	R	J	D	G	F	U	N	K	Y
Y	P	R	P	D	R	D	B	B	G	O	T	E	T	E	Z	G	R	R	X
D	R	S	E	P	J	M	D	N	D	I	S	V	X	D	L	P	U	M	M
M	S	U	F	N	E	S	I	I	U	A	N	K	E	E	M	E	R	U	H
Q	B	L	V	K	E	F	R	S	C	N	R	S	D	E	T	S	H	T	C
K	X	L	J	K	F	R	R	N	K	T	P	F	W	A	R	V	Q	E	Q
C	C	E	S	U	O	E	H	L	A	K	C	M	S	X	E	W	D	N
C	S	N	C	C	P	W	M	H	L	H	V	A	U	L	T	E	D	D	J

A loud burst of noise (4)
A person who does an activity as a hobby instead of for pay (7)
A rundown, low-rent apartment building (8)
Activity engage in regularly; an endeavor (7)
Beating with fists (9)
Calm; unruffled (6)
Continuing without interruption (9)
Dependent on a habit-forming substance (6)
Diligently thought about; focused (12)
Earthy and uncomplicated; natural (5)
Enclosed (7)
Gloomy (6)
Hallway (8)
Hitting with an open hand (7)
Hum-drum; lifelessness; boredom (12)
In a refined manner; classically beautifully (9)
In a trance (10)

Indistinctly; unclearly (7)
Insignia; symbolic badge or design (6)
Jumped (7)
Making unable to move or act (10)
Mixed (7)
Moved shoulders up and down as a gesture of doubt or indifference (8)
Muffled; sound made soft by distance or interference (6)
One employed to drive an automobile (9)
Passed; expired (6)
Restlessly; anxiously (11)
Rolled or pitched suddenly or erratically (7)
Seen as a dark outline against a light background (11)
That which goes before or prepares (11)
Turned towards one side (6)
With reserve; showing decorum; with dignity (9)

Contender Vocabulary Word Search 1 Answer Key

Words are placed backwards, forward, diagonally, up and down. Clues listed below can help you find the words. Circle the hidden vocabulary words in the maze.

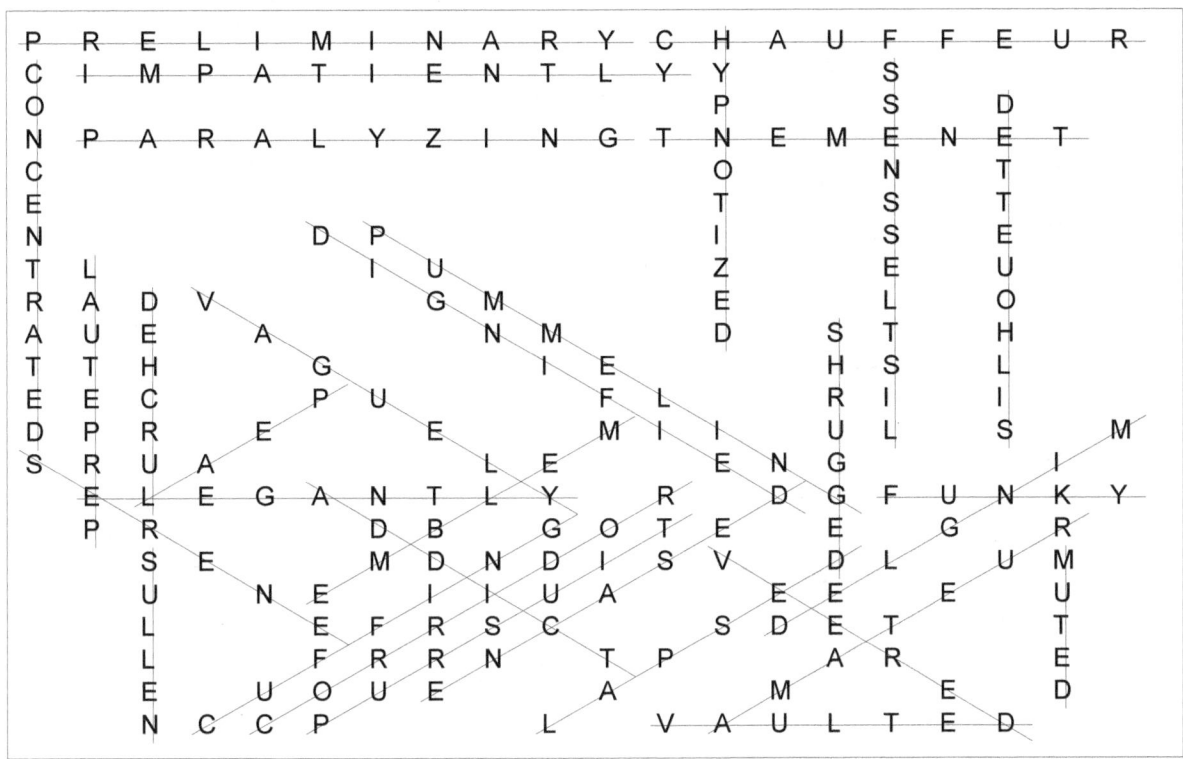

A loud burst of noise (4)
A person who does an activity as a hobby instead of for pay (7)
A rundown, low-rent apartment building (8)
Activity engage in regularly; an endeavor (7)
Beating with fists (9)
Calm; unruffled (6)
Continuing without interruption (9)
Dependent on a habit-forming substance (6)
Diligently thought about; focused (12)
Earthy and uncomplicated; natural (5)
Enclosed (7)
Gloomy (6)
Hallway (8)
Hitting with an open hand (7)
Hum-drum; lifelessness; boredom (12)
In a refined manner; classically beautifully (9)
In a trance (10)

Indistinctly; unclearly (7)
Insignia; symbolic badge or design (6)
Jumped (7)
Making unable to move or act (10)
Mixed (7)
Moved shoulders up and down as a gesture of doubt or indifference (8)
Muffled; sound made soft by distance or interference (6)
One employed to drive an automobile (9)
Passed; expired (6)
Restlessly; anxiously (11)
Rolled or pitched suddenly or erratically (7)
Seen as a dark outline against a light background (11)
That which goes before or prepares (11)
Turned towards one side (6)
With reserve; showing decorum; with dignity (9)

Contender Vocabulary Word Search 2

Words are placed backwards, forward, diagonally, up and down. Clues listed below can help you find the words. Circle the hidden vocabulary words in the maze.

I	M	P	A	T	I	E	N	T	L	Y	C	F	Y	D	S	J	P	Q	T
H	L	C	Z	M	R	P	J	P	P	M	D	W	E	Q	I	L	U	G	P
W	R	L	H	T	V	X	E	T	U	C	Y	G	F	F	L	L	M	S	F
X	Y	B	P	C	E	F	F	R	W	R	G	R	Y	R	H	W	M	S	T
J	R	K	R	I	L	X	S	R	P	U	S	D	J	C	O	Z	E	G	T
C	S	R	E	D	E	X	L	V	R	E	V	U	J	J	U	K	L	V	H
H	D	K	L	D	G	J	I	H	N	B	T	K	I	F	E	J	I	K	H
A	L	J	I	A	A	F	S	C	D	E	N	U	F	T	T	M	N	C	J
U	U	F	M	M	N	Y	T	H	S	T	N	L	A	T	T	I	G	S	P
F	R	N	I	A	T	D	L	K	P	T	E	C	A	L	E	N	M	U	R
F	C	R	N	T	L	G	E	M	M	H	V	N	A	P	D	G	V	L	W
E	H	X	A	E	Y	F	S	G	Y	Y	M	T	E	S	S	L	F	L	G
U	E	Q	R	U	H	J	S	P	D	G	U	V	R	M	E	E	C	E	E
R	D	D	Y	R	C	O	N	C	E	N	T	R	A	T	E	D	D	N	Q
F	B	K	K	O	X	O	E	Q	I	I	E	V	C	G	E	N	E	P	P
X	X	T	F	D	T	C	S	M	F	Z	D	D	A	R	U	R	T	E	P
H	L	G	R	I	R	U	S	J	I	Y	C	E	E	U	E	E	C	A	Z
Q	C	L	Z	R	S	F	S	B	N	L	F	E	M	S	L	Y	L	L	G
B	V	E	H	R	J	F	R	D	G	A	V	U	D	B	Z	T	W	Y	J
Z	D	G	C	O	G	I	X	P	I	R	Z	H	N	M	L	N	E	J	V
R	H	H	R	C	X	N	Z	F	D	A	W	V	F	K	Q	E	X	D	J
K	Y	J	Q	B	C	G	V	W	K	P	G	P	G	C	Y	M	M	M	M

A loud burst of noise (4)
A person who does an activity as a hobby instead of for pay (7)
A rundown, low-rent apartment building (8)
Activity engage in regularly; an endeavor (7)
Beating with fists (9)
Calm; unruffled (6)
Continuing without interruption (9)
Dependent on a habit-forming substance (6)
Diligently thought about; focused (12)
Earthy and uncomplicated; natural (5)
Enclosed (7)
Gloomy (6)
Hallway (8)
Hitting with an open hand (7)
Hum-drum; lifelessness; boredom (12)
In a refined manner; classically beautifully (9)
In a trance (10)

Indistinctly; unclearly (7)
Insignia; symbolic badge or design (6)
Jumped (7)
Making unable to move or act (10)
Mixed (7)
Moved shoulders up and down as a gesture of doubt or indifference (8)
Muffled; sound made soft by distance or interference (6)
One employed to drive an automobile (9)
Passed; expired (6)
Restlessly; anxiously (11)
Rolled or pitched suddenly or erratically (7)
Seen as a dark outline against a light background (11)
That which goes before or prepares (11)
Turned towards one side (6)
With reserve; showing decorum; with dignity (9)

Contender Vocabulary Word Search 2 Answer Key

Words are placed backwards, forward, diagonally, up and down. Clues listed below can help you find the words. Circle the hidden vocabulary words in the maze.

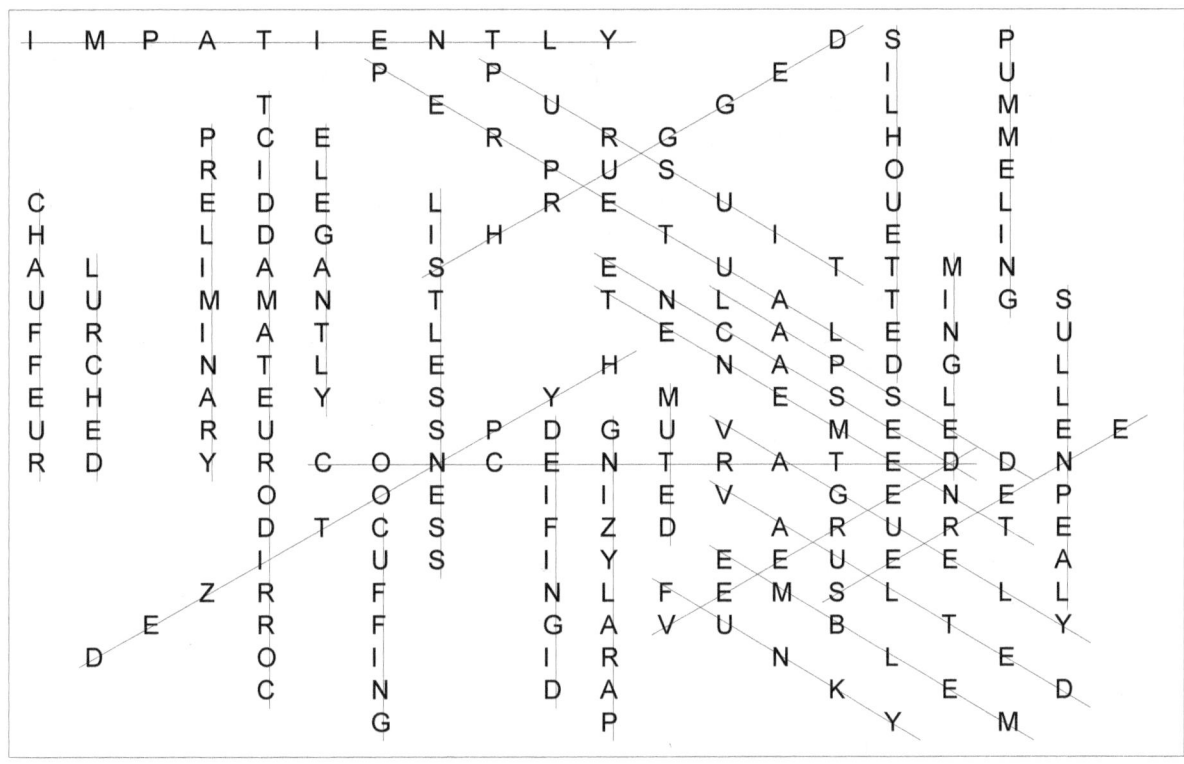

A loud burst of noise (4)
A person who does an activity as a hobby instead of for pay (7)
A rundown, low-rent apartment building (8)
Activity engage in regularly; an endeavor (7)
Beating with fists (9)
Calm; unruffled (6)
Continuing without interruption (9)
Dependent on a habit-forming substance (6)
Diligently thought about; focused (12)
Earthy and uncomplicated; natural (5)
Enclosed (7)
Gloomy (6)
Hallway (8)
Hitting with an open hand (7)
Hum-drum; lifelessness; boredom (12)
In a refined manner; classically beautifully (9)
In a trance (10)

Indistinctly; unclearly (7)
Insignia; symbolic badge or design (6)
Jumped (7)
Making unable to move or act (10)
Mixed (7)
Moved shoulders up and down as a gesture of doubt or indifference (8)
Muffled; sound made soft by distance or interference (6)
One employed to drive an automobile (9)
Passed; expired (6)
Restlessly; anxiously (11)
Rolled or pitched suddenly or erratically (7)
Seen as a dark outline against a light background (11)
That which goes before or prepares (11)
Turned towards one side (6)
With reserve; showing decorum; with dignity (9)

Contender Vocabulary Word Search 3

Words are placed backwards, forward, diagonally, up and down. Words listed below are included in the maze. Circle the hidden vocabulary words in the maze.

```
D I G N I F I E D E T T E U O H L I S G
N Y H P P F K C B F C O R R I D O R L N
Y L D K W B B J L D N C H J S S W R H L
X Y D P D R T V C S R J C J H G W D V Y
M V D E E Q S S V B X P Y R C L G F A J
L S P R H Q E U E T Z K U S U X L Q U V
F I G P C J R L E H D G R T F L T Y L B
U M S E R M E L R T G B T T F V R A T D
N P M T U D N E E E M Q C F I A E J E V
K A Z U L G E N D E Z I T O N P Y H D G
Y T D A Y E E E V C D H N I G B Y E E S
Z I Z L N M S J J D X T M G L F S M T F
Z E V N E P X S A Y J I G C L A T E A J
M N S N A Q G F N L L T C B C E M L R H
U T T L Y J L X P E I Z J N G L D E T N
T L E T L T S J R U S Q E S J P J G N L
E Y Y M R B S P S X S S V Y X K V A E C
D Y S P B L C R U E F F U A H C S N C F
S K K M Q L U V T B Y G G F M L G T N D
X P X Y R P E Y B R Z P N K B L N L O X
V A G U E L Y M P U M M E L I N G Y C Y
P A R A L Y Z I N G A M A T E U R L H J
```

ADDICT	HYPNOTIZED	PUMMELING
AMATEUR	IMPATIENTLY	PURSUIT
CHAUFFEUR	LAPSED	SERENE
CONCENTRATED	LISTLESSNESS	SHRUGGED
CORRIDOR	LURCHED	SILHOUETTED
CUFFING	MINGLED	SULLEN
DIGNIFIED	MUTED	TENEMENT
ELEGANTLY	PARALYZING	VAGUELY
EMBLEM	PEAL	VAULTED
ENCASED	PERPETUAL	VEERED
FUNKY	PRELIMINARY	

Contender Vocabulary Word Search 3 Answer Key

Words are placed backwards, forward, diagonally, up and down. Words listed below are included in the maze. Circle the hidden vocabulary words in the maze.

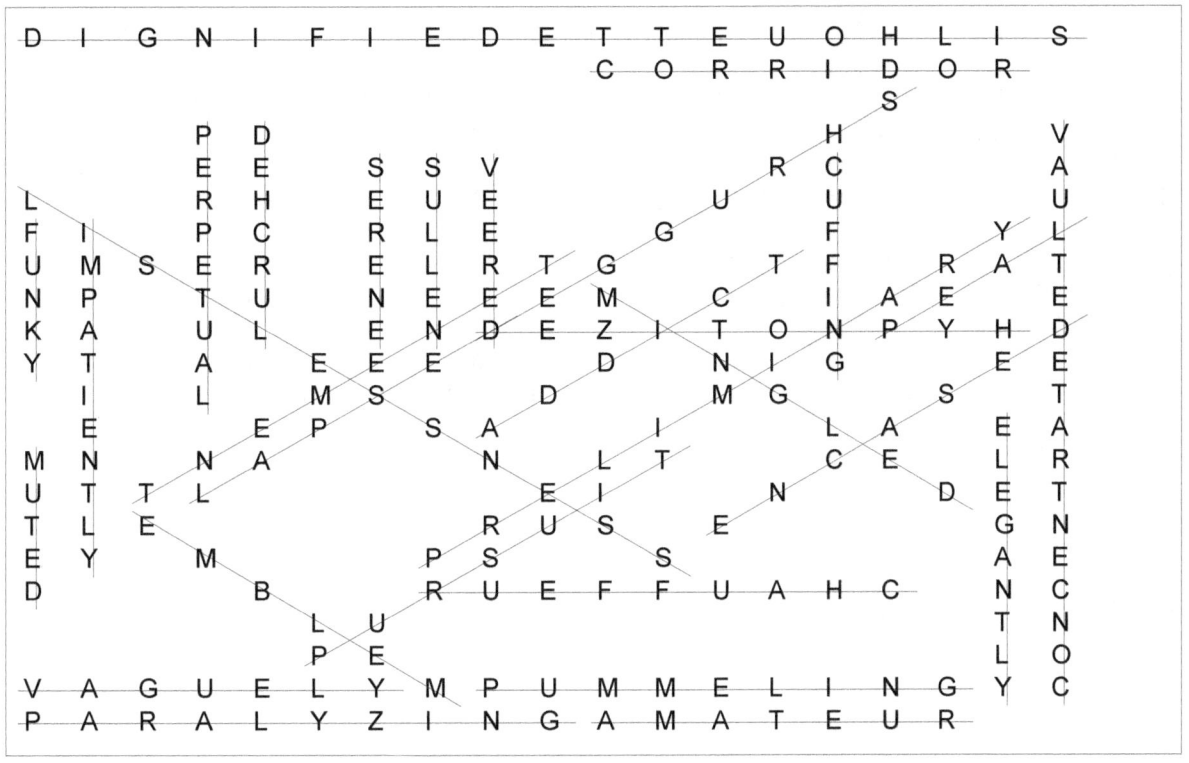

ADDICT	HYPNOTIZED	PUMMELING
AMATEUR	IMPATIENTLY	PURSUIT
CHAUFFEUR	LAPSED	SERENE
CONCENTRATED	LISTLESSNESS	SHRUGGED
CORRIDOR	LURCHED	SILHOUETTED
CUFFING	MINGLED	SULLEN
DIGNIFIED	MUTED	TENEMENT
ELEGANTLY	PARALYZING	VAGUELY
EMBLEM	PEAL	VAULTED
ENCASED	PERPETUAL	VEERED
FUNKY	PRELIMINARY	

Contender Vocabulary Word Search 4

Words are placed backwards, forward, diagonally, up and down. Words listed below are included in the maze. Circle the hidden vocabulary words in the maze.

```
P E R P E T U A L U R C H E D H R Z W F
C L Y C Z S C C M D V T Z G K O R K R P
L I S T L E S S N E S S D N D J G W D S
B M X L J G Z J C H P E M I B D Z D L B
C H A U F F E U R P Z L R L G H W B Y B
D E T T E U O H L I S R Q E X S W K M D
P L V D P F T Q T P O G G M D G C X C R
R Z S R N B G O V C Z L C M J J C O K M
P H W H C F N G J W Z F C U Q T N Y M D
S Y D W R P R C V J Y T G P P C V I P Q
D Y S Z Y U U G N K L X M Q E E N T R D
C S E H S F G E Z M E W U N E G F H E X
H G R L F B P G N W U G T R L L K D L M
T H E I E G A M E C G R E E T C E A I K
F U N K Y G R H Y D A D D I C T P T M F
X G E D Q U A N R T V S E M L S I E I J
P F D B E V L N E S K M E U E U S N N F
K E N T L K Y D T T B R A D S R U E A B
T C A J N N Z P Q L L V K R R X L M R T
F M F L C F I D E C Y V U S P D L E Y H
A Y P D K W N M H H F P D L B N E N H Z
D E I F I N G I D I M P A T I E N T L Y
```

ADDICT	HYPNOTIZED	PUMMELING
AMATEUR	IMPATIENTLY	PURSUIT
CHAUFFEUR	LAPSED	SERENE
CONCENTRATED	LISTLESSNESS	SHRUGGED
CORRIDOR	LURCHED	SILHOUETTED
CUFFING	MINGLED	SULLEN
DIGNIFIED	MUTED	TENEMENT
ELEGANTLY	PARALYZING	VAGUELY
EMBLEM	PEAL	VAULTED
ENCASED	PERPETUAL	VEERED
FUNKY	PRELIMINARY	

Contender Vocabulary Word Search 4 Answer Key

Words are placed backwards, forward, diagonally, up and down. Words listed below are included in the maze. Circle the hidden vocabulary words in the maze.

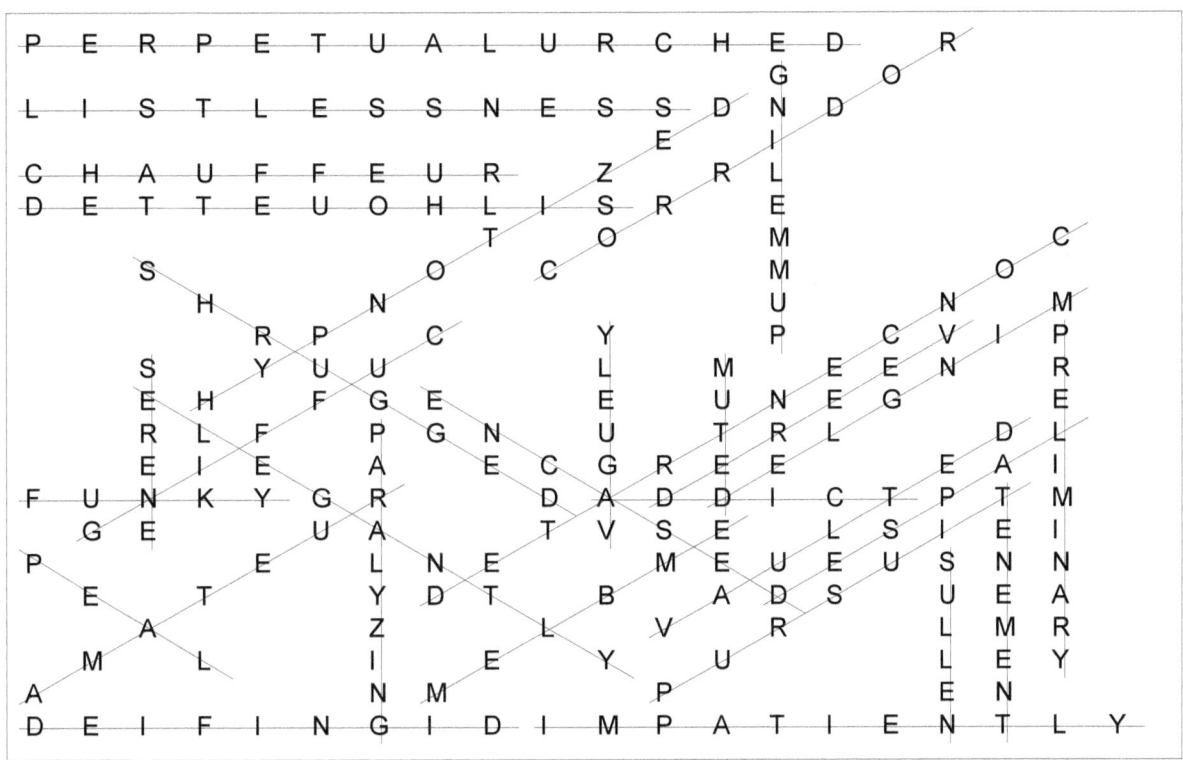

ADDICT	HYPNOTIZED	PUMMELING
AMATEUR	IMPATIENTLY	PURSUIT
CHAUFFEUR	LAPSED	SERENE
CONCENTRATED	LISTLESSNESS	SHRUGGED
CORRIDOR	LURCHED	SILHOUETTED
CUFFING	MINGLED	SULLEN
DIGNIFIED	MUTED	TENEMENT
ELEGANTLY	PARALYZING	VAGUELY
EMBLEM	PEAL	VAULTED
ENCASED	PERPETUAL	VEERED
FUNKY	PRELIMINARY	

Contender Vocabulary Crossword 1

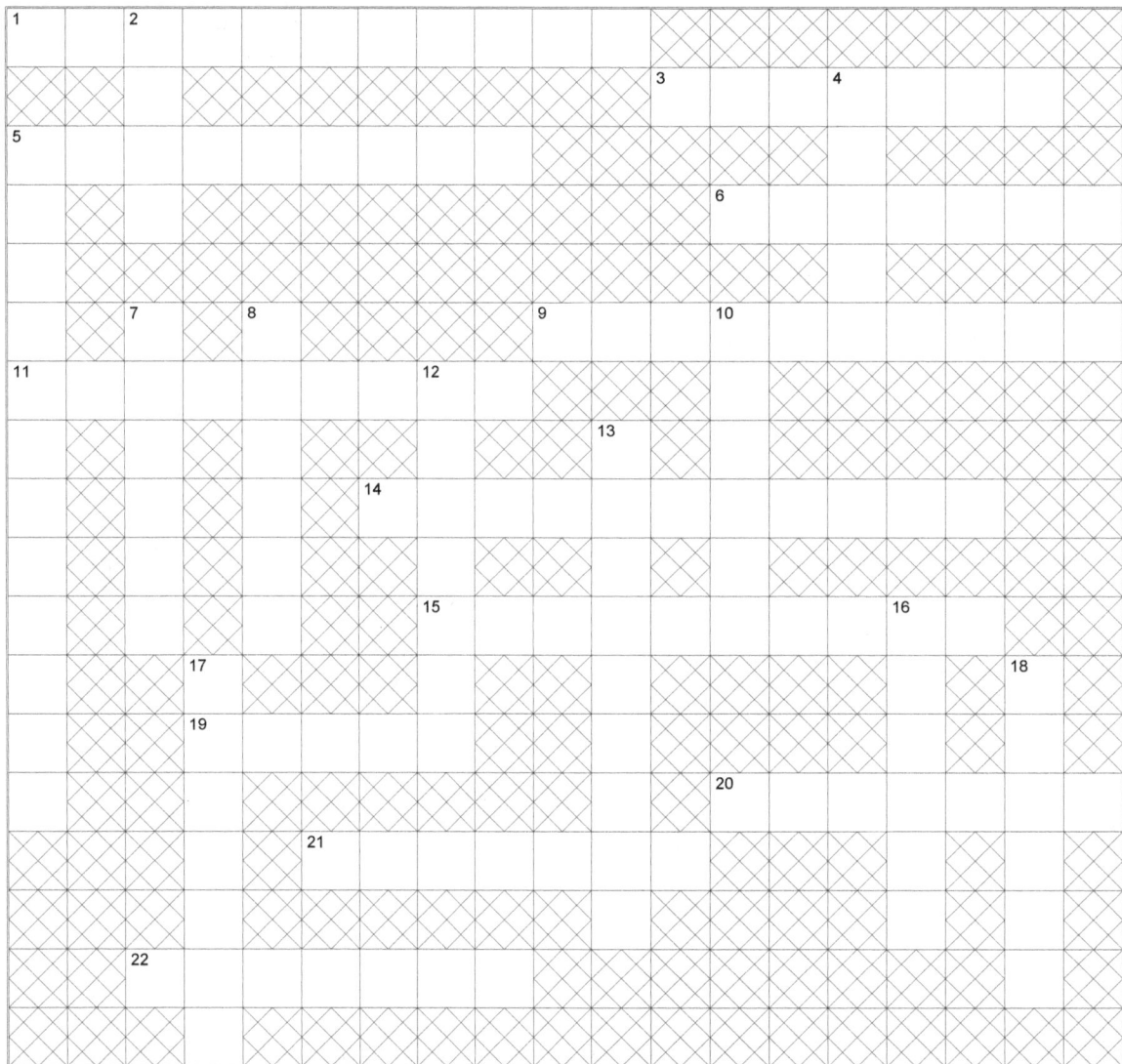

Across
1. Restlessly; anxiously
3. Hitting with an open hand
5. One employed to drive an automobile
6. Mixed
9. Making unable to move or act
11. In a refined manner; classically beautifully
14. That which goes before or prepares
15. In a trance
19. Muffled; sound made soft by distance or interference
20. Jumped
21. Enclosed
22. Activity engage in regularly; an endeavor

Down
2. A loud burst of noise
4. Earthy and uncomplicated; natural
5. Diligently thought about; focused
7. Calm; unruffled
8. Passed; expired
10. Dependent on a habit-forming substance
12. Rolled or pitched suddenly or erratically
13. With reserve; showing decorum; with dignity
16. Insignia; symbolic badge or design
17. A person who does an activity as a hobby instead of for pay
18. Turned towards one side

Contender Vocabulary Crossword 1 Answer Key

Across
1. Restlessly; anxiously
3. Hitting with an open hand
5. One employed to drive an automobile
6. Mixed
9. Making unable to move or act
11. In a refined manner; classically beautifully
14. That which goes before or prepares
15. In a trance
19. Muffled; sound made soft by distance or interference
20. Jumped
21. Enclosed
22. Activity engage in regularly; an endeavor

Down
2. A loud burst of noise
4. Earthy and uncomplicated; natural
5. Diligently thought about; focused
7. Calm; unruffled
8. Passed; expired
10. Dependent on a habit-forming substance
12. Rolled or pitched suddenly or erratically
13. With reserve; showing decorum; with dignity
16. Insignia; symbolic badge or design
17. A person who does an activity as a hobby instead of for pay
18. Turned towards one side

Contender Vocabulary Crossword 2

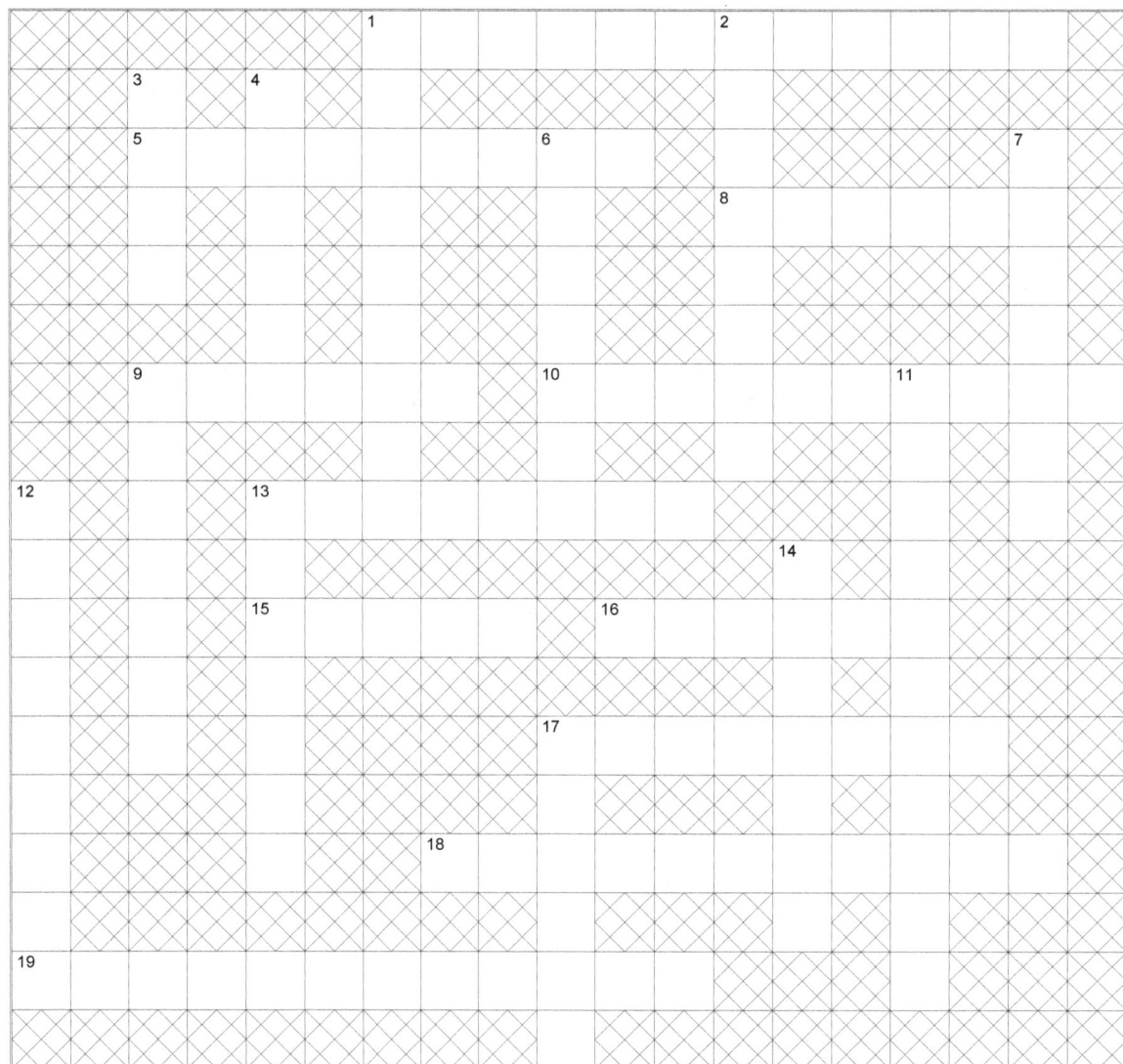

Across
1. Diligently thought about; focused
5. In a refined manner; classically beautifully
8. Insignia; symbolic badge or design
9. Turned towards one side
10. In a trance
13. Hallway
15. Earthy and uncomplicated; natural
16. Dependent on a habit-forming substance
17. Moved shoulders up and down as a gesture of doubt or indifference
18. Seen as a dark outline against a light background
19. Hum-drum; lifelessness; boredom

Down
1. One employed to drive an automobile
2. A rundown, low-rent apartment building
3. A loud burst of noise
4. Calm; unruffled
6. Rolled or pitched suddenly or erratically
7. A person who does an activity as a hobby instead of for pay
9. Jumped
11. Restlessly; anxiously
12. Continuing without interruption
13. Hitting with an open hand
14. Mixed
17. Gloomy

Contender Vocabulary Crossword 2 Answer Key

Across
1. Diligently thought about; focused
5. In a refined manner; classically beautifully
8. Insignia; symbolic badge or design
9. Turned towards one side
10. In a trance
13. Hallway
15. Earthy and uncomplicated; natural
16. Dependent on a habit-forming substance
17. Moved shoulders up and down as a gesture of doubt or indifference
18. Seen as a dark outline against a light background
19. Hum-drum; lifelessness; boredom

Down
1. One employed to drive an automobile
2. A rundown, low-rent apartment building
3. A loud burst of noise
4. Calm; unruffled
6. Rolled or pitched suddenly or erratically
7. A person who does an activity as a hobby instead of for pay
9. Jumped
11. Restlessly; anxiously
12. Continuing without interruption
13. Hitting with an open hand
14. Mixed
17. Gloomy

Contender Vocabulary Crossword 3

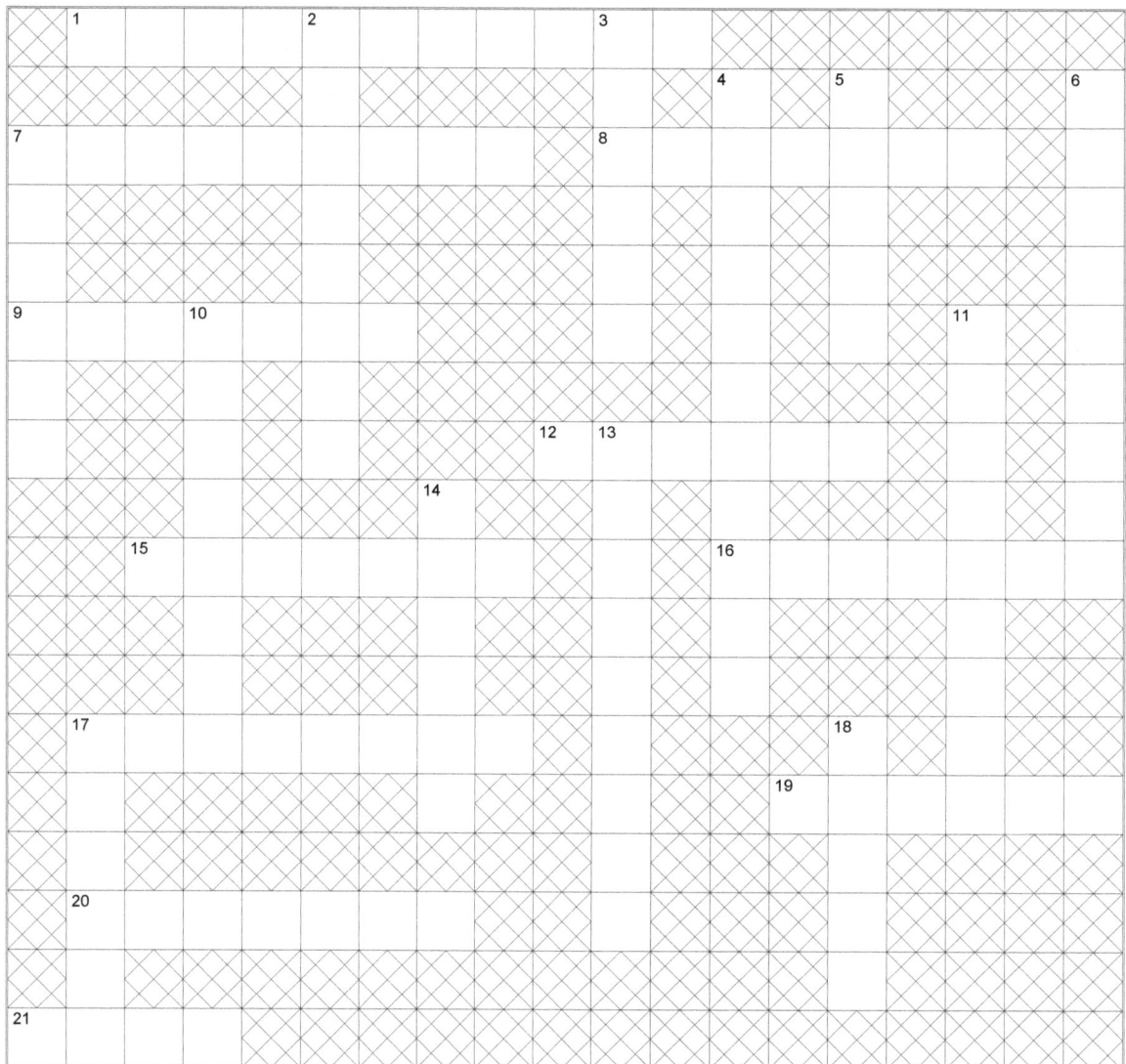

Across
1. Restlessly; anxiously
7. In a refined manner; classically beautifully
8. Activity engage in regularly; an endeavor
9. Rolled or pitched suddenly or erratically
12. Dependent on a habit-forming substance
15. Mixed
16. A person who does an activity as a hobby instead of for pay
17. Moved shoulders up and down as a gesture of doubt or indifference
19. Gloomy
20. Enclosed
21. A loud burst of noise

Down
2. A rundown, low-rent apartment building
3. Passed; expired
4. That which goes before or prepares
5. Muffled; sound made soft by distance or interference
6. One employed to drive an automobile
7. Insignia; symbolic badge or design
10. Hallway
11. Continuing without interruption
13. With reserve; showing decorum; with dignity
14. Turned towards one side
17. Calm; unruffled
18. Earthy and uncomplicated; natural

Contender Vocabulary Crossword 3 Answer Key

		1 I	M	P	2 A	T	I	E	N	T	3 L	Y			
					T E						A		4 P		5 M		6 C
7 E	L	E	G	A	N	T	L	Y	8 P	U	R	S	U	I	T	H
M					E				S		E		T			A
B					M				E		L		E			U
9 L	U	10 R	C	H	E	D			D		I		D		11 P	F
E		O			N						M				E	F
M		R			T			12 A	13 D	D	I	C	T		R	E
		R					14 V		I		N				P	U
		15 M	I	N	G	L	E	D		G		16 A	M	A	T	E	U	R
		D					E			N		R			T	
		O					R			I		Y			U	
		17 S	H	R	U	G	G	E	D		F			18 F	A	
		E					D			I		19 S	U	L	L	E	N
		R								E		N				
		20 E	N	C	A	S	E	D		D		K				
		N										Y				
21 P	E	A	L													

Across
1. Restlessly; anxiously
7. In a refined manner; classically beautifully
8. Activity engage in regularly; an endeavor
9. Rolled or pitched suddenly or erratically
12. Dependent on a habit-forming substance
15. Mixed
16. A person who does an activity as a hobby instead of for pay
17. Moved shoulders up and down as a gesture of doubt or indifference
19. Gloomy
20. Enclosed
21. A loud burst of noise

Down
2. A rundown, low-rent apartment building
3. Passed; expired
4. That which goes before or prepares
5. Muffled; sound made soft by distance or interference
6. One employed to drive an automobile
7. Insignia; symbolic badge or design
10. Hallway
11. Continuing without interruption
13. With reserve; showing decorum; with dignity
14. Turned towards one side
17. Calm; unruffled
18. Earthy and uncomplicated; natural

Contender Vocabulary Crossword 4

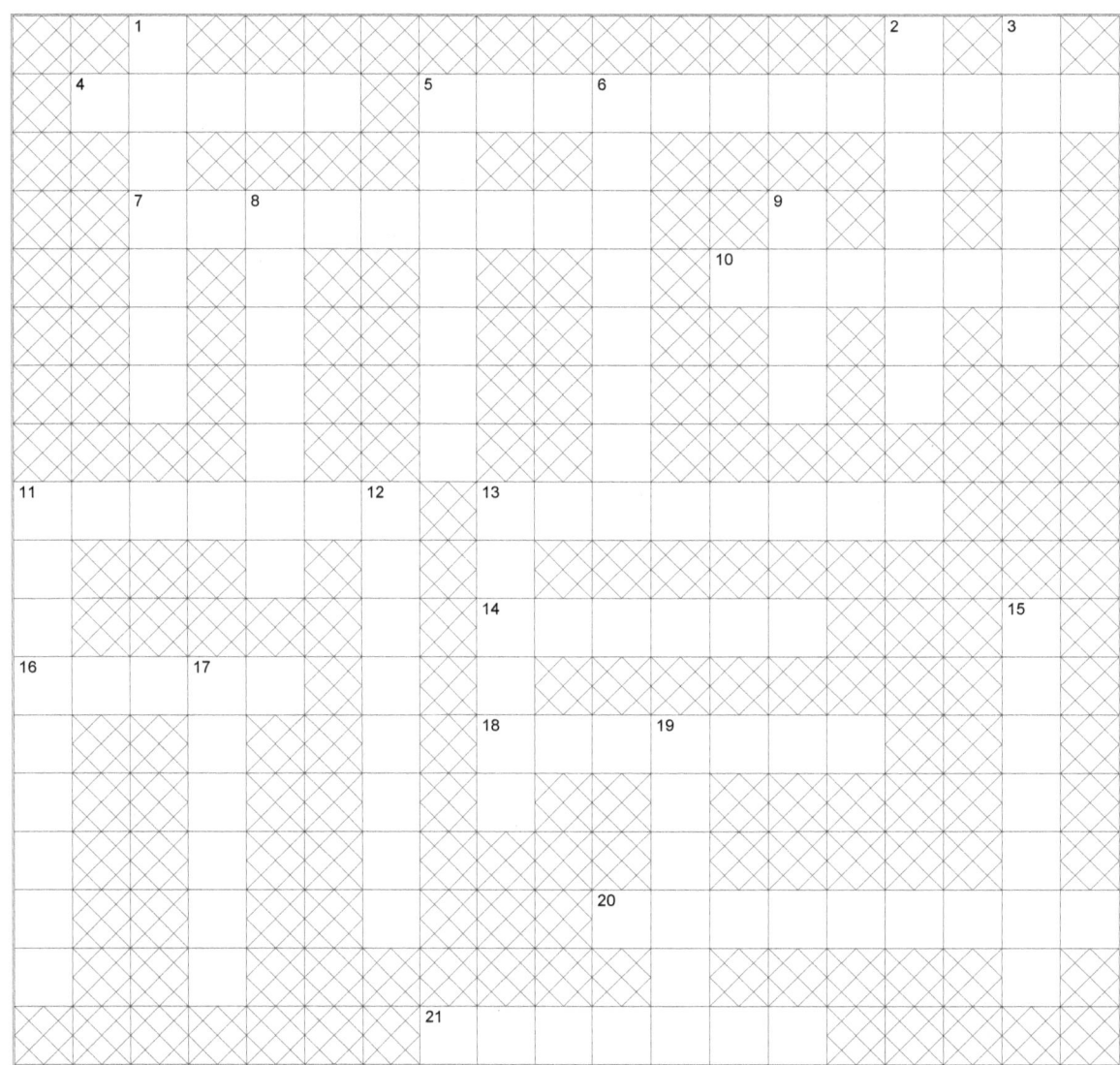

Across
4. Earthy and uncomplicated; natural
5. Diligently thought about; focused
7. One employed to drive an automobile
10. Calm; unruffled
11. Activity engage in regularly; an endeavor
13. Moved shoulders up and down as a gesture of doubt or indifference
14. Passed; expired
16. Muffled; sound made soft by distance or interference
18. Enclosed
20. With reserve; showing decorum; with dignity
21. Jumped

Down
1. Rolled or pitched suddenly or erratically
2. Indistinctly; unclearly
3. Turned towards one side
5. Hitting with an open hand
6. Hallway
8. A person who does an activity as a hobby instead of for pay
9. A loud burst of noise
11. Beating with fists
12. A rundown, low-rent apartment building
13. Gloomy
15. Mixed
17. Insignia; symbolic badge or design
19. Dependent on a habit-forming substance

Contender Vocabulary Crossword 4 Answer Key

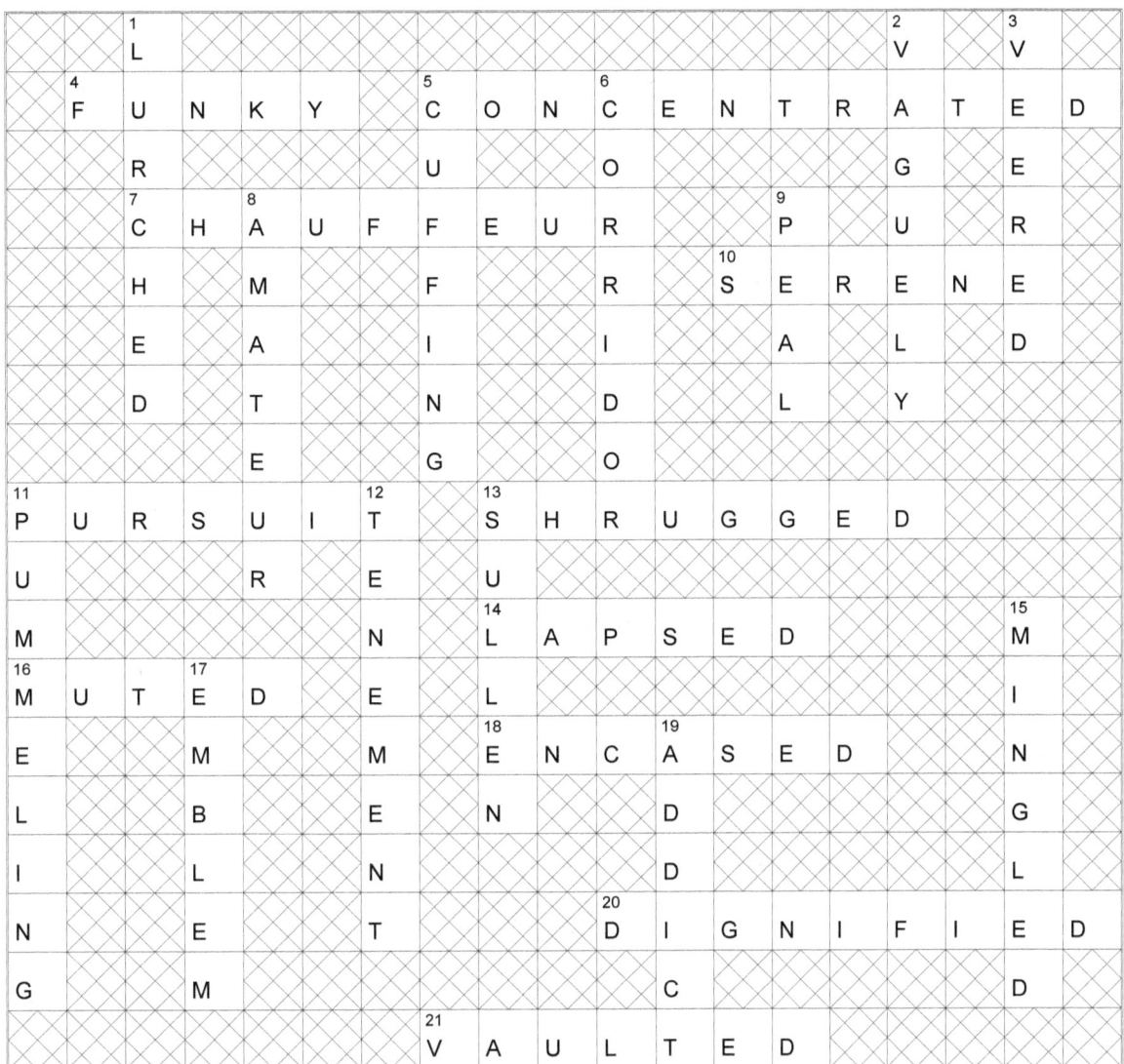

Across
4. Earthy and uncomplicated; natural
5. Diligently thought about; focused
7. One employed to drive an automobile
10. Calm; unruffled
11. Activity engage in regularly; an endeavor
13. Moved shoulders up and down as a gesture of doubt or indifference
14. Passed; expired
16. Muffled; sound made soft by distance or interference
18. Enclosed
20. With reserve; showing decorum; with dignity
21. Jumped

Down
1. Rolled or pitched suddenly or erratically
2. Indistinctly; unclearly
3. Turned towards one side
5. Hitting with an open hand
6. Hallway
8. A person who does an activity as a hobby instead of for pay
9. A loud burst of noise
11. Beating with fists
12. A rundown, low-rent apartment building
13. Gloomy
15. Mixed
17. Insignia; symbolic badge or design
19. Dependent on a habit-forming substance

Contender Vocabulary Juggle Letters 1

1. CDRRIORO = 1. _____
   Hallway

2. APEL = 2. _____
   A loud burst of noise

3. EELPPRUAT = 3. _____
   Continuing without interruption

4. EDREVE = 4. _____
   Turned towards one side

5. NKYUF = 5. _____
   Earthy and uncomplicated; natural

6. ETGYLNLEA = 6. _____
   In a refined manner; classically beautifully

7. ENSACED = 7. _____
   Enclosed

8. UET DM = 8. _____
   Muffled; sound made soft by distance or interference

9. YAUVLEG = 9. _____
   Indistinctly; unclearly

10. NFUGFIC = 10. _____
    Hitting with an open hand

11. DADICT = 11. _____
    Dependent on a habit-forming substance

12. TMARUEA = 12. _____
    A person who does an activity as a hobby instead of for pay

13. ETETNEMN = 13. _____
    A rundown, low-rent apartment building

14. GMULIMPEN = 14. _____
    Beating with fists

15. FDENGDIII = 15. _____
    With reserve; showing decorum; with dignity

Contender Vocabulary Juggle Letters 1 Answer Key

1. CDRRIORO = 1. CORRIDOR
Hallway

2. APEL = 2. PEAL
A loud burst of noise

3. EELPPRUAT = 3. PERPETUAL
Continuing without interruption

4. EDREVE = 4. VEERED
Turned towards one side

5. NKYUF = 5. FUNKY
Earthy and uncomplicated; natural

6. ETGYLNLEA = 6. ELEGANTLY
In a refined manner; classically beautifully

7. ENSACED = 7. ENCASED
Enclosed

8. UET DM = 8. MUTED
Muffled; sound made soft by distance or interference

9. YAUVLEG = 9. VAGUELY
Indistinctly; unclearly

10. NFUGFIC =10. CUFFING
Hitting with an open hand

11. DADICT =11. ADDICT
Dependent on a habit-forming substance

12. TMARUEA =12. AMATEUR
A person who does an activity as a hobby instead of for pay

13. ETETNEMN =13. TENEMENT
A rundown, low-rent apartment building

14. GMULIMPEN =14. PUMMELING
Beating with fists

15. FDENGDIII =15. DIGNIFIED
With reserve; showing decorum; with dignity

Contender Vocabulary Juggle Letters 2

1. MNIULPMGE = 1. _____
   Beating with fists

2. EENRES = 2. _____
   Calm; unruffled

3. DMEUT = 3. _____
   Muffled; sound made soft by distance or interference

4. ACHUFUERF = 4. _____
   One employed to drive an automobile

5. METAURA = 5. _____
   A person who does an activity as a hobby instead of for pay

6. AMPTYIILNTE = 6. _____
   Restlessly; anxiously

7. UEYLVAG = 7. _____
   Indistinctly; unclearly

8. CAIDDT = 8. _____
   Dependent on a habit-forming substance

9. NYUFK = 9. _____
   Earthy and uncomplicated; natural

10. FIIDNEGID = 10. _____
    With reserve; showing decorum; with dignity

11. GDILMEN = 11. _____
    Mixed

12. EESSLLSTNSSI = 12. _____
    Hum-drum; lifelessness; boredom

13. ERTPAPLEU = 13. _____
    Continuing without interruption

14. RRILYEIPNMA = 14. _____
    That which goes before or prepares

15. YOHTPINZED = 15. _____
    In a trance

Contender Vocabulary Juggle Letters 2 Answer Key

1. MNIULPMGE = 1. PUMMELING
Beating with fists

2. EENRES = 2. SERENE
Calm; unruffled

3. DMEUT = 3. MUTED
Muffled; sound made soft by distance or interference

4. ACHUFUERF = 4. CHAUFFEUR
One employed to drive an automobile

5. METAURA = 5. AMATEUR
A person who does an activity as a hobby instead of for pay

6. AMPTYIILNTE = 6. IMPATIENTLY
Restlessly; anxiously

7. UEYLVAG = 7. VAGUELY
Indistinctly; unclearly

8. CAIDDT = 8. ADDICT
Dependent on a habit-forming substance

9. NYUFK = 9. FUNKY
Earthy and uncomplicated; natural

10. FIIDNEGID = 10. DIGNIFIED
With reserve; showing decorum; with dignity

11. GDILMEN = 11. MINGLED
Mixed

12. EESSLLSTNSSI = 12. LISTLESSNESS
Hum-drum; lifelessness; boredom

13. ERTPAPLEU = 13. PERPETUAL
Continuing without interruption

14. RRILYEIPNMA = 14. PRELIMINARY
That which goes before or prepares

15. YOHTPINZED = 15. HYPNOTIZED
In a trance

Contender Vocabulary Juggle Letters 3

1. SLNLEESSTSIS = 1. _____
   Hum-drum; lifelessness; boredom

2. PIYZEOHTDN = 2. _____
   In a trance

3. TIRUPUS = 3. _____
   Activity engage in regularly; an endeavor

4. TUPREAPLE = 4. _____
   Continuing without interruption

5. LUDERHC = 5. _____
   Rolled or pitched suddenly or erratically

6. MMBEEL = 6. _____
   Insignia; symbolic badge or design

7. LTOTEEIHDUS = 7. _____
   Seen as a dark outline against a light background

8. FECAURHUF = 8. _____
   One employed to drive an automobile

9. RDIRORCO = 9. _____
   Hallway

10. RNSEEE = 10. _____
    Calm; unruffled

11. LVAEUGY = 11. _____
    Indistinctly; unclearly

12. ESAPLD = 12. _____
    Passed; expired

13. RUGSGDHE = 13. _____
    Moved shoulders up and down as a gesture of doubt or indifference

14. EDTLVAU = 14. _____
    Jumped

15. EVEDER = 15. _____
    Turned towards one side

Contender Vocabulary Juggle Letters 3 Answer Key

1. SLNLEESSTSIS = 1. LISTLESSNESS
Hum-drum; lifelessness; boredom

2. PIYZEOHTDN = 2. HYPNOTIZED
In a trance

3. TIRUPS = 3. PURSUIT
Activity engage in regularly; an endeavor

4. TUPREAPLE = 4. PERPETUAL
Continuing without interruption

5. LUDERHC = 5. LURCHED
Rolled or pitched suddenly or erratically

6. MMBEEL = 6. EMBLEM
Insignia; symbolic badge or design

7. LTOTEEIHDUS = 7. SILHOUETTED
Seen as a dark outline against a light background

8. FECAURHUF = 8. CHAUFFEUR
One employed to drive an automobile

9. RDIRORCO = 9. CORRIDOR
Hallway

10. RNSEEE = 10. SERENE
Calm; unruffled

11. LVAEUGY = 11. VAGUELY
Indistinctly; unclearly

12. ESAPLD = 12. LAPSED
Passed; expired

13. RUGSGDHE = 13. SHRUGGED
Moved shoulders up and down as a gesture of doubt or indifference

14. EDTLVAU = 14. VAULTED
Jumped

15. EVEDER = 15. VEERED
Turned towards one side

Contender Vocabulary Juggle Letters 4

1. LYZRPIAGAN = 1. _____
   Making unable to move or act

2. BELMME = 2. _____
   Insignia; symbolic badge or design

3. REEDEV = 3. _____
   Turned towards one side

4. EMNTTEEN = 4. _____
   A rundown, low-rent apartment building

5. LTAEYENGL = 5. _____
   In a refined manner; classically beautifully

6. GEIFDIDNI = 6. _____
   With reserve; showing decorum; with dignity

7. TITLOUDESHE = 7. _____
   Seen as a dark outline against a light background

8. LPERUPAET = 8. _____
   Continuing without interruption

9. ESSLLNTESISS = 9. _____
   Hum-drum; lifelessness; boredom

10. DHUELCR =10. _____
    Rolled or pitched suddenly or erratically

11. URAEATM =11. _____
    A person who does an activity as a hobby instead of for pay

12. LLNUES =12. _____
    Gloomy

13. ODPYNHZEIT =13. _____
    In a trance

14. TVULDEA =14. _____
    Jumped

15. LGVUAEY =15. _____
    Indistinctly; unclearly

Contender Vocabulary Juggle Letters 4 Answer Key

1. LYZRPIAGAN = 1. PARALYZING
   Making unable to move or act

2. BELMME = 2. EMBLEM
   Insignia; symbolic badge or design

3. REEDEV = 3. VEERED
   Turned towards one side

4. EMNTTEEN = 4. TENEMENT
   A rundown, low-rent apartment building

5. LTAEYENGL = 5. ELEGANTLY
   In a refined manner; classically beautifully

6. GEIFDIDNI = 6. DIGNIFIED
   With reserve; showing decorum; with dignity

7. TITLOUDESHE = 7. SILHOUETTED
   Seen as a dark outline against a light background

8. LPERUPAET = 8. PERPETUAL
   Continuing without interruption

9. ESSLLNTESISS = 9. LISTLESSNESS
   Hum-drum; lifelessness; boredom

10. DHUELCR =10. LURCHED
    Rolled or pitched suddenly or erratically

11. URAEATM =11. AMATEUR
    A person who does an activity as a hobby instead of for pay

12. LLNUES =12. SULLEN
    Gloomy

13. ODPYNHZEIT =13. HYPNOTIZED
    In a trance

14. TVULDEA =14. VAULTED
    Jumped

15. LGVUAEY =15. VAGUELY
    Indistinctly; unclearly

ADDICT	Dependent on a habit-forming substance
AMATEUR	A person who does an activity as a hobby instead of for pay
CHAUFFEUR	One employed to drive an automobile
CONCENTRATED	Diligently thought about; focused
CORRIDOR	Hallway
CUFFING	Hitting with an open hand

DIGNIFIED	With reserve; showing decorum; with dignity
ELEGANTLY	In a refined manner; classically beautifully
EMBLEM	Insignia; symbolic badge or design
ENCASED	Enclosed
FUNKY	Earthy and uncomplicated; natural
HYPNOTIZED	In a trance

IMPATIENTLY	Restlessly; anxiously
LAPSED	Passed; expired
LISTLESSNESS	Hum-drum; lifelessness; boredom
LURCHED	Rolled or pitched suddenly or erratically
MINGLED	Mixed
MUTED	Muffled; sound made soft by distance or interference

PARALYZING	Making unable to move or act
PEAL	A loud burst of noise
PERPETUAL	Continuing without interruption
PRELIMINARY	That which goes before or prepares
PUMMELING	Beating with fists
PURSUIT	Activity engage in regularly; an endeavor

SERENE	Calm; unruffled
SHRUGGED	Moved shoulders up and down as a gesture of doubt or indifference
SILHOUETTED	Seen as a dark outline against a light background
SULLEN	Gloomy
TENEMENT	A rundown, low-rent apartment building
VAGUELY	Indistinctly; unclearly

VAULTED	Jumped
VEERED	Turned towards one side

Contender Vocabulary

LAPSED	SILHOUETTED	ADDICT	PURSUIT	PARALYZING
PEAL	SHRUGGED	FUNKY	EMBLEM	LISTLESSNESS
HYPNOTIZED	CONCENTRATED	FREE SPACE	TENEMENT	PRELIMINARY
SERENE	IMPATIENTLY	ELEGANTLY	VEERED	CHAUFFEUR
VAULTED	SULLEN	VAGUELY	AMATEUR	MUTED

Contender Vocabulary

LURCHED	MINGLED	CUFFING	PERPETUAL	CORRIDOR
PUMMELING	DIGNIFIED	MUTED	AMATEUR	VAGUELY
SULLEN	VAULTED	FREE SPACE	VEERED	ELEGANTLY
IMPATIENTLY	SERENE	PRELIMINARY	TENEMENT	ENCASED
CONCENTRATED	HYPNOTIZED	LISTLESSNESS	EMBLEM	FUNKY

Contender Vocabulary

PEAL	HYPNOTIZED	MUTED	PERPETUAL	AMATEUR
IMPATIENTLY	LAPSED	SILHOUETTED	ENCASED	SULLEN
ADDICT	LURCHED	FREE SPACE	PRELIMINARY	MINGLED
VEERED	VAGUELY	PUMMELING	SERENE	EMBLEM
FUNKY	CHAUFFEUR	DIGNIFIED	TENEMENT	SHRUGGED

Contender Vocabulary

CORRIDOR	PARALYZING	LISTLESSNESS	PURSUIT	CONCENTRATED
ELEGANTLY	CUFFING	SHRUGGED	TENEMENT	DIGNIFIED
CHAUFFEUR	FUNKY	FREE SPACE	SERENE	PUMMELING
VAGUELY	VEERED	MINGLED	PRELIMINARY	VAULTED
LURCHED	ADDICT	SULLEN	ENCASED	SILHOUETTED

Contender Vocabulary

SERENE	HYPNOTIZED	LAPSED	DIGNIFIED	SHRUGGED
LURCHED	PRELIMINARY	PUMMELING	PEAL	PURSUIT
CORRIDOR	ADDICT	FREE SPACE	SULLEN	FUNKY
AMATEUR	ELEGANTLY	CONCENTRATED	ENCASED	IMPATIENTLY
CUFFING	VAGUELY	LISTLESSNESS	MINGLED	SILHOUETTED

Contender Vocabulary

CHAUFFEUR	PARALYZING	PERPETUAL	TENEMENT	EMBLEM
MUTED	VEERED	SILHOUETTED	MINGLED	LISTLESSNESS
VAGUELY	CUFFING	FREE SPACE	ENCASED	CONCENTRATED
ELEGANTLY	AMATEUR	FUNKY	SULLEN	VAULTED
ADDICT	CORRIDOR	PURSUIT	PEAL	PUMMELING

Contender Vocabulary

DIGNIFIED	LAPSED	VAGUELY	CHAUFFEUR	SHRUGGED
LURCHED	PARALYZING	PEAL	ADDICT	SILHOUETTED
TENEMENT	EMBLEM	FREE SPACE	VAULTED	SERENE
LISTLESSNESS	CORRIDOR	PERPETUAL	ENCASED	PRELIMINARY
MUTED	VEERED	FUNKY	ELEGANTLY	PURSUIT

Contender Vocabulary

CONCENTRATED	IMPATIENTLY	HYPNOTIZED	PUMMELING	AMATEUR
SULLEN	MINGLED	PURSUIT	ELEGANTLY	FUNKY
VEERED	MUTED	FREE SPACE	ENCASED	PERPETUAL
CORRIDOR	LISTLESSNESS	SERENE	VAULTED	CUFFING
EMBLEM	TENEMENT	SILHOUETTED	ADDICT	PEAL

Contender Vocabulary

SILHOUETTED	PEAL	AMATEUR	MINGLED	FUNKY
LAPSED	LISTLESSNESS	LURCHED	VAGUELY	CHAUFFEUR
ELEGANTLY	CORRIDOR	FREE SPACE	SHRUGGED	PERPETUAL
PUMMELING	SULLEN	ADDICT	IMPATIENTLY	EMBLEM
VAULTED	CONCENTRATED	PARALYZING	VEERED	MUTED

Contender Vocabulary

DIGNIFIED	PRELIMINARY	SERENE	PURSUIT	ENCASED
CUFFING	TENEMENT	MUTED	VEERED	PARALYZING
CONCENTRATED	VAULTED	FREE SPACE	IMPATIENTLY	ADDICT
SULLEN	PUMMELING	PERPETUAL	SHRUGGED	HYPNOTIZED
CORRIDOR	ELEGANTLY	CHAUFFEUR	VAGUELY	LURCHED

Contender Vocabulary

FUNKY	LISTLESSNESS	VAULTED	MINGLED	VAGUELY
CONCENTRATED	LURCHED	SHRUGGED	IMPATIENTLY	PARALYZING
CUFFING	ENCASED	FREE SPACE	PEAL	ADDICT
SILHOUETTED	SERENE	PRELIMINARY	AMATEUR	DIGNIFIED
EMBLEM	SULLEN	ELEGANTLY	MUTED	HYPNOTIZED

Contender Vocabulary

VEERED	LAPSED	CORRIDOR	TENEMENT	PUMMELING
PURSUIT	CHAUFFEUR	HYPNOTIZED	MUTED	ELEGANTLY
SULLEN	EMBLEM	FREE SPACE	AMATEUR	PRELIMINARY
SERENE	SILHOUETTED	ADDICT	PEAL	PERPETUAL
ENCASED	CUFFING	PARALYZING	IMPATIENTLY	SHRUGGED

Contender Vocabulary

AMATEUR	PRELIMINARY	TENEMENT	VAGUELY	LAPSED
MUTED	CUFFING	LURCHED	FUNKY	SULLEN
VAULTED	DIGNIFIED	FREE SPACE	PURSUIT	ADDICT
SHRUGGED	PARALYZING	CHAUFFEUR	PEAL	SILHOUETTED
LISTLESSNESS	ENCASED	CONCENTRATED	HYPNOTIZED	ELEGANTLY

Contender Vocabulary

SERENE	EMBLEM	PUMMELING	CORRIDOR	VEERED
PERPETUAL	MINGLED	ELEGANTLY	HYPNOTIZED	CONCENTRATED
ENCASED	LISTLESSNESS	FREE SPACE	PEAL	CHAUFFEUR
PARALYZING	SHRUGGED	ADDICT	PURSUIT	IMPATIENTLY
DIGNIFIED	VAULTED	SULLEN	FUNKY	LURCHED

Contender Vocabulary

PEAL	CHAUFFEUR	SULLEN	CONCENTRATED	AMATEUR
PERPETUAL	CORRIDOR	FUNKY	EMBLEM	SHRUGGED
LISTLESSNESS	MINGLED	FREE SPACE	MUTED	LAPSED
PUMMELING	SERENE	CUFFING	VAULTED	TENEMENT
IMPATIENTLY	DIGNIFIED	VEERED	PURSUIT	LURCHED

Contender Vocabulary

PRELIMINARY	ELEGANTLY	HYPNOTIZED	PARALYZING	ADDICT
VAGUELY	SILHOUETTED	LURCHED	PURSUIT	VEERED
DIGNIFIED	IMPATIENTLY	FREE SPACE	VAULTED	CUFFING
SERENE	PUMMELING	LAPSED	MUTED	ENCASED
MINGLED	LISTLESSNESS	SHRUGGED	EMBLEM	FUNKY

Contender Vocabulary

SULLEN	IMPATIENTLY	VAGUELY	PEAL	MINGLED
EMBLEM	TENEMENT	LURCHED	DIGNIFIED	AMATEUR
VAULTED	PARALYZING	FREE SPACE	LISTLESSNESS	FUNKY
SHRUGGED	HYPNOTIZED	SERENE	PUMMELING	ELEGANTLY
LAPSED	SILHOUETTED	PERPETUAL	CORRIDOR	CUFFING

Contender Vocabulary

PRELIMINARY	ENCASED	CHAUFFEUR	ADDICT	MUTED
PURSUIT	CONCENTRATED	CUFFING	CORRIDOR	PERPETUAL
SILHOUETTED	LAPSED	FREE SPACE	PUMMELING	SERENE
HYPNOTIZED	SHRUGGED	FUNKY	LISTLESSNESS	VEERED
PARALYZING	VAULTED	AMATEUR	DIGNIFIED	LURCHED

Contender Vocabulary

MUTED	SERENE	ADDICT	PRELIMINARY	MINGLED
FUNKY	VAGUELY	AMATEUR	ENCASED	CHAUFFEUR
CORRIDOR	EMBLEM	FREE SPACE	ELEGANTLY	PARALYZING
CUFFING	PERPETUAL	PURSUIT	HYPNOTIZED	LISTLESSNESS
SILHOUETTED	LAPSED	VAULTED	TENEMENT	CONCENTRATED

Contender Vocabulary

IMPATIENTLY	DIGNIFIED	SHRUGGED	SULLEN	LURCHED
PEAL	PUMMELING	CONCENTRATED	TENEMENT	VAULTED
LAPSED	SILHOUETTED	FREE SPACE	HYPNOTIZED	PURSUIT
PERPETUAL	CUFFING	PARALYZING	ELEGANTLY	VEERED
EMBLEM	CORRIDOR	CHAUFFEUR	ENCASED	AMATEUR

Contender Vocabulary

PEAL	CHAUFFEUR	PARALYZING	MINGLED	TENEMENT
ELEGANTLY	AMATEUR	SERENE	MUTED	LISTLESSNESS
PERPETUAL	DIGNIFIED	FREE SPACE	EMBLEM	VEERED
CORRIDOR	PRELIMINARY	SHRUGGED	FUNKY	HYPNOTIZED
LURCHED	IMPATIENTLY	CONCENTRATED	CUFFING	ADDICT

Contender Vocabulary

ENCASED	PURSUIT	VAULTED	PUMMELING	SULLEN
SILHOUETTED	LAPSED	ADDICT	CUFFING	CONCENTRATED
IMPATIENTLY	LURCHED	FREE SPACE	FUNKY	SHRUGGED
PRELIMINARY	CORRIDOR	VEERED	EMBLEM	VAGUELY
DIGNIFIED	PERPETUAL	LISTLESSNESS	MUTED	SERENE

Contender Vocabulary

VAULTED	VAGUELY	CONCENTRATED	MUTED	CORRIDOR
LAPSED	SILHOUETTED	PEAL	PURSUIT	SHRUGGED
ENCASED	PERPETUAL	FREE SPACE	ELEGANTLY	PUMMELING
FUNKY	HYPNOTIZED	SERENE	LURCHED	AMATEUR
MINGLED	VEERED	IMPATIENTLY	TENEMENT	DIGNIFIED

Contender Vocabulary

LISTLESSNESS	PRELIMINARY	PARALYZING	SULLEN	ADDICT
CHAUFFEUR	CUFFING	DIGNIFIED	TENEMENT	IMPATIENTLY
VEERED	MINGLED	FREE SPACE	LURCHED	SERENE
HYPNOTIZED	FUNKY	PUMMELING	ELEGANTLY	EMBLEM
PERPETUAL	ENCASED	SHRUGGED	PURSUIT	PEAL

Contender Vocabulary

ELEGANTLY	SERENE	LAPSED	AMATEUR	CONCENTRATED
HYPNOTIZED	PEAL	SHRUGGED	DIGNIFIED	SILHOUETTED
VEERED	CORRIDOR	FREE SPACE	CUFFING	MUTED
LISTLESSNESS	PUMMELING	PRELIMINARY	PURSUIT	PERPETUAL
ENCASED	EMBLEM	VAGUELY	LURCHED	IMPATIENTLY

Contender Vocabulary

PARALYZING	ADDICT	SULLEN	TENEMENT	CHAUFFEUR
MINGLED	VAULTED	IMPATIENTLY	LURCHED	VAGUELY
EMBLEM	ENCASED	FREE SPACE	PURSUIT	PRELIMINARY
PUMMELING	LISTLESSNESS	MUTED	CUFFING	FUNKY
CORRIDOR	VEERED	SILHOUETTED	DIGNIFIED	SHRUGGED

Contender Vocabulary

SULLEN	ADDICT	LURCHED	SERENE	PUMMELING
PEAL	PARALYZING	PURSUIT	MINGLED	MUTED
CORRIDOR	DIGNIFIED	FREE SPACE	PERPETUAL	VAGUELY
ELEGANTLY	PRELIMINARY	IMPATIENTLY	LISTLESSNESS	AMATEUR
EMBLEM	SHRUGGED	FUNKY	CONCENTRATED	VEERED

Contender Vocabulary

TENEMENT	CHAUFFEUR	HYPNOTIZED	ENCASED	SILHOUETTED
LAPSED	CUFFING	VEERED	CONCENTRATED	FUNKY
SHRUGGED	EMBLEM	FREE SPACE	LISTLESSNESS	IMPATIENTLY
PRELIMINARY	ELEGANTLY	VAGUELY	PERPETUAL	VAULTED
DIGNIFIED	CORRIDOR	MUTED	MINGLED	PURSUIT

Contender Vocabulary

PARALYZING	SULLEN	CONCENTRATED	LISTLESSNESS	SHRUGGED
PEAL	CUFFING	PERPETUAL	PURSUIT	MINGLED
DIGNIFIED	HYPNOTIZED	FREE SPACE	LURCHED	VAULTED
AMATEUR	MUTED	VAGUELY	VEERED	FUNKY
ENCASED	TENEMENT	IMPATIENTLY	SILHOUETTED	ELEGANTLY

Contender Vocabulary

CHAUFFEUR	SERENE	PRELIMINARY	LAPSED	EMBLEM
CORRIDOR	PUMMELING	ELEGANTLY	SILHOUETTED	IMPATIENTLY
TENEMENT	ENCASED	FREE SPACE	VEERED	VAGUELY
MUTED	AMATEUR	VAULTED	LURCHED	ADDICT
HYPNOTIZED	DIGNIFIED	MINGLED	PURSUIT	PERPETUAL

Contender Vocabulary

ADDICT	VAGUELY	CUFFING	SERENE	SHRUGGED
PRELIMINARY	DIGNIFIED	LAPSED	FUNKY	ENCASED
CHAUFFEUR	SILHOUETTED	FREE SPACE	LURCHED	PURSUIT
MINGLED	PEAL	CORRIDOR	PARALYZING	VEERED
AMATEUR	ELEGANTLY	IMPATIENTLY	PERPETUAL	TENEMENT

Contender Vocabulary

EMBLEM	CONCENTRATED	LISTLESSNESS	VAULTED	SULLEN
HYPNOTIZED	PUMMELING	TENEMENT	PERPETUAL	IMPATIENTLY
ELEGANTLY	AMATEUR	FREE SPACE	PARALYZING	CORRIDOR
PEAL	MINGLED	PURSUIT	LURCHED	MUTED
SILHOUETTED	CHAUFFEUR	ENCASED	FUNKY	LAPSED

www.ingramcontent.com/pod-product-compliance
Lightning Source LLC
LaVergne TN
LVHW081538060526
838200LV00048B/2133